Managing Stress At Work
In A Week

Stephen Evans-Howe

The Teach Yourself series has been trusted around the world for over 60 years. This series of 'In A Week' business books is designed to help people at all levels and around the world to fur... he experts learn in

D0582998

Stephen Evans-Howe is a Chartered Safety Practitioner and has held a number of senior management and executive roles in a variety of engineering and service environments: petrochemical, aviation, theme parks and defence. He continues to work in industry, leading the implementation of people-based programmes, supporting safety and organizational culture change.

Teach Yourself®

Managing Stress At Work

Stephen
Evans-Howe

www.inaweek.co.uk

Contents

Introduction

It has been said 'employees join great organizations but leave because of bad managers' and from my own experience I can testify to the truth of the statement.

A number of factors, such as recognition, variety of work, achievement and prospects for promotion play an important role in job satisfaction and help good managers retain their staff. However, stress can be one of the most significant reasons for employees leaving or if not in a position to leave, at least wishing they could.

Some see stress as a problem for the individual or even a sign of some defect in character. Yet most forward-thinking managers and organizations see the effective management of stress as an essential part of their business practice, benefiting both employees and the business or organization.

This book is written for managers as a simple, practical guide to the principles and techniques for managing stress at work. It looks at stress from an organizational perspective as well as highlighting practical steps individual managers can take to enable them to gain competitive advantage through effective management of their most valuable asset – their people. Even if you have no direct line-management responsibilities now, you can use what you have learnt to influence decision-makers, perhaps even your own line manager, to better manage stress in the workplace.

Arguably anyone who comes into contact with another person needs to manage stress. Whether in the workplace, socially or at home, human interaction can create pressures, conflict and stress. Even when free from the influence of others we can often generate our own stress through our own desire to succeed or through innate fears and concerns.

Over the years I have worked in a variety of safety critical environments, including petrochemical, aviation and theme park industries, and while stress can have a detrimental effect on morale, staff recruitment and retention I have seen how failure to effectively manage stress can lead to human error with catastrophic consequences.

This book will help you understand what stress is, why we get stressed and some of its physiological and psychological symptoms. You will learn about some of the background research into the psychology of stress and consider a variety of theories and models. More importantly, with this simple guidance, practical techniques and some relevant examples you will be able to create a challenging and supportive environment where people know what is expected, work hard, avoid burnout and make a real impact in your organization. You will also be able to spot issues and resolve problems before they become significant. By effectively managing stress at work you will be able to reduce the burden of sickness absence, poor productivity, high staff turnover and workplace injury and liability claims.

As well as managing the stress of others at work, you will also find some useful tips and suggestions that you can adopt to take personal charge of your own stress levels, allowing you to relax, keep healthy and stay on top.

Ultimately how you handle stress personally and as a manager will vary depending on a number of factors: types of people, the organization, inherent pressures of a job and specific economic factors. This book aims to provide you with information that you can use in assessing what is appropriate for you, your team and organization.

At the end of each chapter you will find ten multiple choice questions. Their aim is to support your learning rather than act as a pass or fail test, and I do encourage you to try them.

I hope you enjoy reading this book and I wish you every success in applying what you learn.

What is stress?

We have all heard people saying they are stressed – you may even have said it yourself. Perhaps you have had a lot on at work or too much to think about or maybe others are making unreasonable demands on your time. In this chapter you will learn that the response to stress is hard-wired into our biology and has played an important role in the survival of the human race. We will look at how the modern world can confuse or trigger our natural response to danger and understand that what we call stress today isn't always bad, isn't the same for everyone and that stress can exist even if there are no visible signs of it.

We will also look at how to assess stress in the workplace, consider the causes of stress that can be generated by organizations, other circumstances in our lives and even by our own outlook and expectations. Finally, we will examine some of the impacts stress can have on both individuals and organizations and in turn demonstrate the real value of the effective management of stress.

What is stress?

If you ask a group of individuals what they mean by stress, you will find some people talk about the causes of stress, giving responses such as 'too much work', 'too much pressure', while others will respond citing the effects of stress, with responses such as 'feeling tired or depressed'. For clarity, throughout this book we will refer to the causes of stress as **stressors** and the effects as the **response.**

The stress response

Stress is a commonly used word but one that means different things to different people and lacks a single coherent definition. At a basic level stress relates to the biological response of our body to certain situations.

Throughout pre-history people faced life and death situations on a daily basis with strong competition for survival. Since the earliest days of the human race, an inbuilt stress response has proved to be an effective means of protection in situations of extreme danger.

So from a biological perspective, stress is the natural physical reaction to events that make an individual feel threatened in some way. Sometimes the threat is real, such as coming face to face with a predator, or sometimes the threat is imagined – e.g. the wind moving the bushes may cause you to believe there is a predator hiding, ready to pounce. Stress is the body's way of helping to deal with the situation. In the emergency situation stress can save your life as your body automatically adapts to stay focused, alert and highly energized. This acute stress response, often referred to as **fight or flight** (or sometimes the 'fight, flight or freeze response'), prepares the body for fending off an attacker or rival or for running away. The response can also result in freezing to the spot, unable to move.

The response is triggered by a threat, excitement, noise, bright lights or temperature and is characterized by physical changes in the body including the release of hormones such as adrenaline and cortisol. Adrenalin regulates heart rate and the flow of blood and air, by altering the diameter of blood vessels and air passages, while cortisol increases blood sugar, suppresses the immune system and increases metabolism. This chemical/hormonal change triggers the physical changes in the body. Once the threat has passed the body returns to its normal state ready for the next time.

The fight or flight response is directly associated with the autonomic system, which controls both the physiological and psychological change in the body in response to a stressor. We will look at this system in more detail tomorrow.

General adaptation syndrome

Stressors lead to stress and some form of physiological or psychological reaction. In 1936 Austrian-born physician Dr Hans Selye defined his general adaptation syndrome (GAS) as comprising three stages.

1 the **alarm reaction stage**, where a shock stimulates the body's defences
2 the **resistance stage**, where the body either resists the stressor or adapts to the effects of the stressor

3 the **exhaustion phase**, where if the stressor continues but the resistance or adaptation is lost, the body is overloaded, the alarm stage returns and if the stress is prolonged, damage will occur.

Stress in the modern world

Some see GAS as over-simplistic and have developed their thinking to consider a more interactional approach, considering the individual in more detail. Whereas GAS seems to imply an automatic response, research has shown that individuals balance the demands made on them considering a variety of factors and this approach leads to a definition of stress as more of an imbalance.

Factors associated with the interactive model of stress that affect an individual's response include:

● **cognitive appraisal** – an individual's perception of a situation or event
● **experience** – familiarity, previous/historical exposure to similar events, relevant learning or training and any reinforcement or conditioning (what is seen as success or failure to cope)
● **demand** – perceived demand, actual ability to meet demands
● **interpersonal influences** – background and influencing factors
● **state of stress imbalance** – between actual and perceived demand and the ability to cope.

The interactive model provides a useful foundation for the management strategies detailed in later chapters.

Fight or flight evolved for dealing with physical danger in the modern work environment. Today, the situation is more likely to result in psychological danger, anticipation of events such as losing a job, failing to meet a deadline as well as actual danger from bullying or harassment. The world has moved on from the threat of being eaten by a tiger but as yet our biology has not caught up; it doesn't distinguish between physical and psychological threats – just think back to the last time you went to see a horror movie.

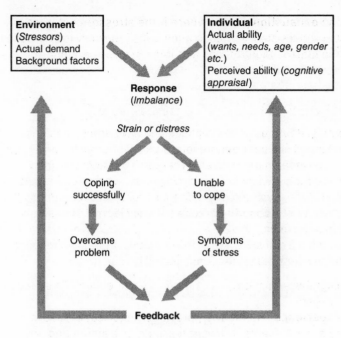

The interactive model of stress

So from a work or organizational perspective, what we mean by stress today is more accurately described as *the negative effects or response to excessive pressure or other types of demands placed on people.*

Stress isn't always bad

Stress can be both positive and negative. Much of this book focuses on management of the negative aspects of stress. However, the benefits of positive stress or pressure should not be overlooked. Positive pressure can be motivating and create a sense of team that helps get the job done.

The effects of positive stress, such as the 'butterfly feeling' you get in your stomach, link back to the basic biological response of fight or flight and the response to hormones in the bloodstream. In small doses this can help you perform under pressure and motivate you to do your best. Think of feelings you may have had before a job interview, a critical presentation or a looming deadline or target. Positive stress can make you feel pumped up and ready to succeed. Managed effectively in the workplace it can improve performance and bring a team together and improve overall wellbeing.

Like all stress though, people's thresholds vary and beyond a certain point stress stops being helpful and can start to damage the body. If you are continually performing under pressure your body and mind will ultimately pay the price.

The human performance curve shows the relationship between stress and performance and is adapted from the Yerkes-Dodson Law, originally developed in the early twentieth century by psychologist Robert M. Yerkes and John Dodson. The law states that performance increases with physiological or mental arousal, but only up to a point. When levels of arousal become too high, performance decreases. The adapted human performance curve illustrates how the same variation in performance is related to the amount of stress to which an individual is exposed.

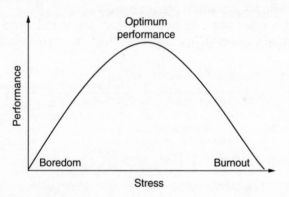

Adapted human performance curve

Stress isn't the same for everyone

Stress can be caused by a variety of stressors, including work situations (e.g. time pressure, fear of redundancy, overwork, bullying, and lack of tools and equipment) or personal experience such as home life or marriage breakdown. No two people react in the same way or to the same degree to a particular stressor. Some people seem to roll with the punches while others crumble at the slightest obstacle.

Earlier we introduced GAS and the idea that adaptation is required to respond to a stressor and that this can be expanded to consider factors relating to the individual – e.g. strength both physically and psychologically, perception and degree of control.

Various psychologists have researched the types and traits of personality or disposition. In Table 1.1 we consider six personality types, their preferred stress state and their vulnerability to the negative effects of excessive stress.

You might recognize some of the personality types in yourself or your work colleagues, although research concludes that most people combine traits of more than one personality type so this information should only be used as a guide for individuals. Good managers realize that people are far more complex than any single model can show and will use this information to build an overall picture of an individual and wouldn't jump to conclusions about who fits into which precise category.

Age, gender and a number of other factors influence an individual's vulnerability to stress. The four important factors

Table 1.1 Disposition and vulnerability to stress

Type	Definition	Preferred stress level	Vulnerability to stress
Ambitious	Strong desire for success or achievement	High	High
Calm	Tranquil, placid and does not easily become disturbed, agitated or excited	Moderate/ Low	Low
Conscientious	Meticulous and takes great care over everything	Low/ Moderate	Moderate (high during change)
Non-assertive	Difficulty in standing up for themselves	Moderate/ Low	Moderate
Lively	Full of vigour, experiences mental and emotional vigour	High	Low (high if pressure from self)
Anxious	Worried and tense, concerned about possible misfortune	Low	High

of control, predictability, expectation and support provide an initial understanding of what controls might be appropriate to combat stress, and we will consider these further later in the week.

Control

If you have the ability to influence events (control the stressor) and meet the specific challenge it is easier to handle stress. This may be a result of your position/level of authority, experience and freedom within an organization. Older people with secure finances may feel they ultimately can walk away or not have to put up with the pressure. This in itself allows them to cope better.

Predictability

An individual is likely to feel greater stress if they are unable to predict the behaviour or occurrence of a stressor. For example, bullying is notoriously unpredictable in terms of knowing what the bully will do next. Predictability is linked with familiarity, knowledge and preparation. An effective technique employed by hospitals to reduce patient stress is to provide an option for patients to familiarize themselves with the hospital surroundings and timetable of events prior to an operation or giving birth. Think about the value of fire drills in preparation for a real emergency situation.

Expectation

People have expectations of their own ability to cope, as well as societal pressures. For example, men have traditionally been seen as breadwinners and so men may be more vulnerable to stress relating to financial pressures. Women on the other hand have traditionally been seen as carers so may appear to be tasked with caring for sick or elderly relatives as well as the stressor of raising a family. These expectations may also be impacted by perception of whether things are or are likely to start getting better.

Support

People who feel they have support, including support from colleagues, managers, unions, friends, family or doctors, are less likely to be affected by stress. Those who take comfort from some form of spiritual support, faith or belief system might also find it easier to cope.

Assessment of stress

In order to identify the signs of stress in the workplace and determine the magnitude of its impact, a manager or organization can start by analysing, using existing performance measures such as sickness absence, accident rates, productivity and quality metrics (customer complaints, volume of rework, etc.). Generally a high degree of stress in the workplace will have a detrimental impact on these measures.

You may also be able to pick up on individuals showing signs of stress such as increased medication, smoking or alcohol use, nail biting or grinding of teeth. People often lose their sense of humour, become touchy or you might sense a general 'negative air' or 'atmosphere' in the workplace. Personal appearance and levels of grooming or personal hygiene may also get worse.

In order to gain a complete picture it is necessary, and in some countries a legal requirement, to make a formal assessment of stress.

Before an assessment takes place it is important to prepare by securing senior management and wider organizational support and buy-in, explaining the potential benefits and that everyone should be involved in the process. This might be seen as a significant change in the organization and we deal with the issues associated with change management on Friday.

The formal assessment process is broken down as follows.

1. Identify potential stressors
Think about the potential causes of stress within the organization, using the information from this book but also think specifically about the type of organization you are in and draw on your own and others' experiences.

2. Identify who is at risk
Gather data, such as any existing performance measures as described above. Get feedback through a survey or questionnaire. Various templates for benchmarking surveys or questionnaires exist and having read the remainder of this book you will no doubt be able to create something that suits your organization.

3. Evaluate the risk
Having collected the data, what does it tell you? Do any existing controls or practices have an impact? Which areas do you need to focus on? It is important to focus on preventing stress but you should also consider mitigation when stress does arise. How is stress identified, escalated and managed?

4. Create an action plan
Create and communicate an action plan showing what will be done, by whom and when. Make sure the actions are followed up and completed.

5. Monitor and review
Periodically check to make sure actions are effective. Regularly review the sources of data, perhaps redoing the survey if you feel it is necessary. You should review at regular intervals but also be aware of any changes within the organization (e.g.

downsizing, introducing new equipment or work patterns)
that may prompt an additional review or the need for
improved controls.

No signs doesn't mean no stress

Regardless of what you have already learnt, a critical thing
to remember is people are often good at hiding stress. This
may be through fear or embarrassment, or perhaps driven
by the culture of an organization. Alternatively it may be an
individual's desire not to let the team down or feeling they have
everything under control or they may simply be blocking it out.

So just because your organization and the individuals within
it may look stress-free doesn't necessarily mean that is actually
the case – more often than not the opposite is true, with a calm
façade hiding the turmoil beneath. Think of a swan gliding
gracefully across a lake: the calm vision isn't the true picture as
beneath the waters its feet are flapping away like crazy.

Causes and impacts of stress

While an organization and work itself can cause stress, not all
stress is work-related and individuals often bring their own
stress into the workplace.

Individual stressors from outside work may overlap with
those at work, such as financial problems at home linking
with reduced hours or pay and job uncertainty. Old style
management that says 'leave your worries at the gate' is no
longer acceptable or effective. Forward thinking employers see
the benefit in providing a sympathetic response, some flexibility
or additional support for individuals with personal stress.

In the workplace stressors can be categorized into several
groups. Understanding these causes of stress by definition will
inform the type of controls that may be effective, which we will
look at from Tuesday onward.

● job roles, responsibility and control, i.e. the actual requirements
of a job role, level of ambiguity in what is expected, any conflict
of interest and the degree of autonomy or control

Table 1.2 The Holmes-Rahe stress scale of life-changing units (LCU)

Life event	LCU	Life event	LCU
Death of a spouse	100	Change in responsibilities at work	29
Divorce	73	Child leaving home	29
Marital separation	65	Trouble with in-laws	29
Imprisonment	63	Outstanding personal achievement	28
Death of a close family member	63	Spouse starts or stops work	26
Personal injury or illness	53	Begin or end school	26
Marriage	50	Change in living conditions	25
Dismissal from work	47	Revision of personal habits	24
Marital reconciliation	45	Trouble with boss	23
Retirement	45	Change in working hours or conditions	20
Change in health of family member	44	Change in residence	20
Pregnancy	40	Change in schools	20
Sexual difficulties	39	Change in recreation	19
Gain a new family member	39	Change in social activities	18
Business readjustment	39	Minor mortgage or loan	17
Change in financial state	38	Change in sleeping habits	16
Death of a close friend	37	Change in number of family reunions	15
Change to different line of work	36	Change in eating habits	15
Change in frequency of arguments	35	Vacation	13
Major mortgage	32	Christmas	12
Foreclosure of mortgage or loan	30	Minor violation of law	11

- workload and work pressure, the characteristic of the task, the capacity of individuals, equipment and processes and both the amount and type of work being undertaken
- the work environment, including the physical environment, space, lighting, heating and ventilation
- behaviour, conflict and support (interpersonal factors). These are associated with relationships between staff and management but also the organizational environment, how well or otherwise the organization is managed and its culture. Also included is the approach to harassment and bullying and level of support available, how people are recognized and how poor performance and behaviours are managed along with specific individual concerns
- change management and how the organization handles changes, from installing new equipment to dealing with growth or downsizing including redundancies.

It is clear from this list that some stressors might be easy to change with minimal effort, others are harder to address and some impossible.

In the late 1960s two researchers, Dr Thomas Holmes and Dr Richard Rahe, identified a relationship between life events and illness. Their results, commonly known as the Holmes-Rahe stress scale, show the relative impact of life events in life-changing units (LCU) (see Table 1.2).

The LCU scores in the table are based on averages from the study. Using the stress scale, a score of 300 or more places an individual at high risk of illness, a score of 150–299 at moderate risk, and less than 150 only at slight risk of illness.

Summary

Today you have covered a lot of ground, so well done. You started by understanding the difference between stressors (the causes of stress) and the response (the effects of stress) and went on to learn about the fight or flight response, general adaptation syndrome and how in today's world we consider an interactive model for stress, considering the individual as well as the surrounding environment.

You learnt the principle of assessing stress in the workplace and how stress isn't always bad and can, in small doses, help improve performance. You saw that stress isn't the same for everyone and factors such as personality, control, predictability, expectations and the level of support available all play a part in how an individual may respond. You also learnt that stress can exist even if there are no visible signs.

You covered the main categories of stress in the workplace, which we will visit through the remainder of the book.

Finally you saw how events in our personal life can overlap with work and how these events can vary in intensity and the impact they have on health.

SUNDAY

MONDAY

TUESDAY

WEDNESDAY

THURSDAY

FRIDAY

SATURDAY

Questions [Answers at the back]

1. Which of the following is not an appropriate description of stress?
   a) The natural biological response to a threat or danger ❑
   b) The series of reactions to a stressor: alarm, resistance or adaptation and potential exhaustion ❑
   c) The negative effects or response to excessive pressure or other types of demands ❑
   d) The way weak people respond in a crisis with panic and confusion ❑

2. Which of the following is a true statement about stress?
   a) The signs of stress can always be seen ❑
   b) Some stress can be positive ❑
   c) Everyone reacts the same way when faced with a life-changing event ❑
   d) Jolly people tend to be less stressed than miserable ones ❑

3. Which of the following personality types may be the most vulnerable to stress?
   a) Ambitious ❑
   b) Calm ❑
   c) Conscientious ❑
   d) Non-assertive ❑

4. What important factors might affect the vulnerability of an individual to stress?
   a) Expectation ❑
   b) Predictability ❑
   c) Level of control ❑
   d) All of the above ❑

5. In the interactive model, which of these factors does not have an effect?
   a) An individual's perception of a situation or event ❑
   b) Whether the threat is physical or psychological in nature ❑
   c) Experience, previous exposure or relevant training ❑
   d) Perceived or actual ability to meet demands ❑

6. What might happen to sickness absence, accidents and customer complaints if a workforce is subject to stress?
   a) They are likely to remain unchanged ❑
   b) They are likely to decrease ❑
   c) They are likely to increase ❑
   d) Measuring these kind of things is irrelevant and a waste of money ❑

7. When assessing stress in the workplace what is the first thing you should do?
   a) Put together an action plan ❑
   b) Assess who might be at risk ❑
   c) Gain support and buy-in from senior managers ❑
   d) Send out a questionnaire ❑

8. When might you revisit your assessment of stress in the workplace?
a) Regularly or if the organization is about to or is going through change ☐
b) When human resources ask for a good news story for the company website ☐
c) If the survey results are bad ☐
d) Just before your performance review so you can show your boss how effective you've been ☐

9. Using the Holmes-Rahe stress scale, which of these events has the greatest impact in terms of life-changing units (LCU)?
a) Change in sleeping habits ☐
b) Pregnancy ☐
c) Change in line of work ☐
d) Marriage ☐

10. What might an organization do to support people with stress relating to their personal life?
a) Be sympathetic, show flexibility and provide support ☐
b) Give them a good talking to so they get a sense of perspective and move on ☐
c) Reduce their overtime or cut their hours so they have time to deal with personal matters ☐
d) All of the above ☐

Understanding stress – some basic psychological and physiological aspects

Yesterday you learnt what stress is, the different models of stress and how in threatening situations the body reacts. Today we will look in more detail at the way the body responds to stress.

We will consider physical and psychological symptoms and the autonomic nervous system's effect on the body as part of the natural stress response. Then we will learn about some of the medical conditions that may be found in the workforce and diagnosed as a result of personal issues or experiences at work. These conditions include anxiety, depression, phobias and post-traumatic stress disorder. Finally we will see how stress can negatively affect an organization.

The aim of the chapter is not to make you a medical expert but to provide a basic understanding of some of the signs and symptoms of stress and how these link to biological processes in the body. You will be able to use this understanding to see warning signs in yourself and work colleagues and also be able to support those with diagnosed medical conditions in your organization.

Effects of stress

The effects of stress on the individual will vary from person to person but will broadly fall into two categories:

- **physiological effects** – the short-term and long-term effects on the body
- **psychological effects** – how people think, feel and behave (also termed cognitive, emotional and behavioural effects).

The following lists give some commons signs and symptoms of stress. The more you notice in yourself or others the closer you or they may be to a stress imbalance or burnout. Bear in mind that the signs and symptoms of stress can also be caused by other medical problems so wherever possible you should seek or encourage others to seek professional medical assistance.

Physiological signs and symptoms

Physiological signs and symptoms are short-term or long-term health effects, and can include the following:

- headaches
- nervous twitches
- memory problems
- mental ill health
- tiredness or sleeping problems
- frequent colds
- breathlessness
- chest pains, rapid heart beat
- high blood pressure and high cholesterol
- heart disease
- stroke
- feeling sick, nauseous or dizzy, fainting
- a craving for food or loss of appetite
- constipation or diarrhoea
- indigestion or heartburn
- diabetes
- gastric ulcers
- cramps or pins and needles
- arthritis
- sexual problems, lack of libido
- susceptibility to some types of cancer.

Psychological signs and symptoms

Psychological signs and symptoms involve how people may think, feel or behave, and include the following:

- anxiety
- fearing the future
- irritable, short temper or aggressive
- seeing only the negative
- frustration
- depressed, generally unhappy
- poor/irrational judgement
- inability to relax
- feeling overwhelmed

- feeling neglected, alone or uncared for
- breakdown in relationships
- job dissatisfaction
- restlessness, agitation, inability to concentrate or relax
- believing you are a failure, bad or ugly
- lack of interest in others
- loss of sense of humour
- avoid making decisions or difficult situations
- deny there is a problem
- reliance on alcohol, cigarettes or drugs to relax
- nervous habits, nail biting, pacing.

The autonomic system

Yesterday we learnt how the fight or flight response is linked to the body's autonomic system. In this system two sets of nerves are responsible for the automatic and unconscious regulation of the body's functions. The sympathetic system prepares the body to fight and the parasympathetic system is concerned with protection of the body with both systems acting in balance. For example, the sympathetic system causes rapid heart rate and breathing while slowing digestion, and the parasympathetic system in contrast reduces heart rate and breathing while increasing digestion. As you will see from the summary of autonomic responses in Table 2.1, it is the body's natural response that causes many of the basic signs and symptoms of stress.

In addition to these general symptoms, certain chronic conditions may arise, with those listed below being the most common although other disorders exist. Specific advice for individuals will be available as a result of formal diagnosis. Whether you see symptoms of these disorders in yourself or others, professional help should be encouraged.

Depression

Depression is a state of low mood, associated with an aversion to activity and feelings of sadness, worry, restlessness and guilt.

Table 2.1 Effects of the autonomic system

Body part/ organ	Effect of parasympathetic system	Effect of sympathetic system
Brain	Reduced neural activity	Increased neural activity, quick decision-making
Heart	Decreased heart rate and output	Increased heart rate and output
Lungs	Breathing slowed	Airways increased, breathing rapid
Liver	Storage of glucose and fat	Breakdown of glucose and fat for energy
Spleen	Retains red blood cells	Contracts and empties red blood cells into the circulation
Digestion	Increased	Decreased
Kidney	Urine production	Reduced urine production
Eyes	Closed, pupils small	Open, pupils dilated
Mouth	Saliva produced	Saliva reduced, dry mouth
Ears	Hearing less acute	Hearing more acute
Skin	Dry, hair flaccid/normal	Sweating, hairs erect
Muscles	Relaxed	Tense
Blood	Normal ability to clot	Increased ability to clot

Depression may also be related to the presence of factors such as:

- family or personal history of depression
- life-changing events such as death of a child or spouse
- drug or alcohol misuse
- chronic pain or illness.

A depressed mood is not necessarily a medical or psychiatric disorder in its own right but in some cases may arise as a side effect to some medical treatments or as a result of some infections or illnesses. Depression can also be the main symptom of some psychiatric disorders, including major depression (also called clinical depression) bipolar disorder (also called manic depression) and seasonal affective disorder where episodes of depression follow a seasonal cycle.

Anxiety

Anxiety is a feeling of unease, apprehension, worry and fear. Many people will feel anxiety at some point in their lives, particularly in response to a dangerous situation or disruptive life events as described yesterday in the Holmes-Rahe stress scale. Anxiety is a perfectly natural response but can develop into a number of conditions.

Generalized anxiety disorder (GAD)

Generalized anxiety disorder arises from feeling anxious over a prolonged period of time rather than in response to a specific event. It can cause both physical and psychological symptoms as described above, and can have a significant impact on daily life. Treatments are available, including a variety of therapies and medication.

Panic disorder

Panic disorder is diagnosed when sufferers experience panic attacks on a regular basis. A panic attack is an overwhelming fear or apprehension and may be accompanied by physical symptoms such as nausea, sweating and palpitations (irregular heart beat). Sufferers may experience as little as one or two panic attacks per month while others may experience them at a frequency of several per week.

Attacks can occur at any time and without warning but may also be related to a particular situation or location. Although intense and frightening, attacks do not cause any physical harm. Treatment is usually by psychological therapies and or medication.

Phobias

Phobias are a fear response that is out of proportion to the risk posed by a particular object, animal or situation. People can gain an irrational fear of almost anything: heights, enclosed spaces, flying, spiders, snakes, clowns or the number 13. The level of anxiety may vary between sufferers, ranging from mild anxiety to a severe panic attack. Sufferers will often go out of their way to avoid all contact with the source of their anxiety, meaning it can have a significant disruptive effect on people's lives.

Those with simple phobias, such as fear of snakes, may be treated by gradual exposure to the animal, object or place, and over time, in incremental steps, sufferers can become desensitized. This can be done using self-help techniques or through professional help. Those with more complex phobias such as agoraphobia (fear of situations where escape might be difficult or help may not be available in an emergency), where an individual may be scared of public transport or may not even be able to leave their house, can be treated over a much longer period of time. Treatment will normally involve therapies such as counselling, psychotherapy or cognitive behavioural therapy (CBT).

Post-traumatic stress disorder (PTSD)

PTSD is an anxiety disorder triggered by a specific frightening or distressing event, including:

- wars, military combat
- terrorism attacks or being held hostage
- natural disasters such as floods or earthquakes
- witnessing violent deaths or serious crimes.

PTSD can develop immediately after the trigger event or become apparent weeks, months or even years later. Sufferers relive the event through flashbacks and nightmares and may experience feelings of guilt and isolation and become irritable and have trouble sleeping.

Treatment depends on the severity of symptoms and how soon they occur after the trigger event. Trauma-focused CBT as well as medication and other psychological treatments may be used.

As you might expect, certain types of work may expose people to greater risk of PTSD: those in the emergency services, armed forces or those who work with the potential threat of physical violence such as prison workers, some civil service positions (e.g. welfare and benefits workers) or even teachers of young adults. In addition to the work people undertake in your organization you should consider their working history as certain industries tend to attract those from a particular background as a second career – e.g. those with military service may be recruited by security or defence firms. In such situations you may consider additional training for staff to be aware of symptoms, and proactively consider support provisions.

Obsessive compulsive disorder (OCD)

OCD is an anxiety disorder characterized by ritualistic behaviours designed to fend off the cause of apprehension, fear or worry. Symptoms include excessive hand washing, cleaning or repeated checking. Some sufferers have a preoccupation with sexual, violent or religious thoughts and others exhibit an aversion to a particular number.

OCD is sometimes linked to high intelligence and sufferers often exhibit other personality disorders. It can be treated by a variety of behavioural therapies and medication. In extreme cases surgical options may be considered.

Other biological considerations

A circadian rhythm is any biological process that follows a 24-hour cycle and can be found across the natural world in plants, animals and fungi. Fundamentally, circadian rhythms are hard-wired into our bodies; however, they can be adjusted to the local environment by external causes. In humans the rhythm is most evident in sleeping and feeding patterns but can also be seen in regulation of core body temperature, brainwave activity, hormone production and cell regeneration.

Circadian rhythms are important when it comes to work patterns, particularly shift working or people who travel extensively crossing multiple time zones – e.g. airline pilots and crew. Inability to following usual sleeping patterns can lead to fatigue, disorientation or insomnia.

To mitigate the impact of shift work it is important to avoid rapid shift changes and permanent night shifts. Minimizing the number of consecutive nights worked and offsetting working time with clear days away from work will all help.

Individuals can also improve their ability to sleep during the day by avoiding alcohol, heavy foods and exercise prior to sleep.

In addition to circadian rhythms the body may also be affected by other temporal cycles such as seasonal changes including reduced daylight hours. In the workplace there may be practical things you can do to accommodate these variations, such as varying lighting types and intensity.

Understand the signs of your own stress

We often see things in others, while failing to recognize the very same things in ourselves. As an individual it is important to consider what stressors trigger a specific reaction in you and what symptoms the response generates, whether they be physical changes or shifts in our feelings, thoughts or behaviour.

By reflecting and taking time to appreciate our own level of stress we can see early warning signs and ensure that we take appropriate action so that symptoms do not become serious and we manage the situation.

We will consider simple steps that everyone can take to reduce stress and improve their general wellbeing on Saturday.

Effects of stress on an organization

In addition to the effect on individuals, stress, irrespective of the cause (either generated by the workplace or brought in by an individual from their personal life) can have a significant impact on an organization. The effects of stress on an organization can include:

- employee loyalty and commitment to work
- employee recruitment and retention
- employee performance and productivity
- accident rates, sickness absence and customer complaints
- customer satisfaction
- reputation, brand and image.

In some situations, where an organization is the cause of stress, employers may also face legal responsibilities and failure to manage stress may result in regulatory action or litigation resulting in prosecution and or compensation claims.

Like individuals, organizations also vary in their vulnerability to stress, with certain occupations or organizations more prone by the nature of the work done. These might include the emergency services; teaching; work that involves a high degree of uncertainty or interaction with public or societal groups who themselves may be under stress, so employees become on the receiving end of others' fight or flight response; shift or night workers, where their diurnal rhythms are impacted; those who perform safety critical roles where errors may have catastrophic consequences, such as air traffic controllers.

Remember that if you decide to take action to manage stress, you must prepare individuals and organizations, as you do not want your efforts to backfire and cause additional pressure/demands on others. You will also need to be conscious that not all management techniques are appropriate for all organizations.

Summary

Today you have learnt some of the psychological and physiological symptoms of stress as well as the link between these symptoms and the autonomic system's effect on a variety of organs and parts of the body.

You saw some of the common medical conditions associated with stress, and how circadian rhythms and seasonal cycles can impact the body and what steps may be taken to manage them. You should understand the importance of self-awareness in terms of what triggers stress for you personally so you can help manage your own stress levels.

Finally you saw how stress in the workplace can negatively impact an organization through reduced employee loyalty, commitment to work, performance and productivity, increased accidents and sickness absence rates, low customer satisfaction and damage to an organization's reputation and brand. Organizations should also be aware of any specific regulatory requirement associated with the management of stress to avoid potential prosecutions or compensation claims.

SUNDAY
MONDAY
TUESDAY
WEDNESDAY
THURSDAY
FRIDAY
SATURDAY

Questions [Answers at the back]

1. Which of the symptoms below is not a potential physical sign of stress?
   a) Headaches ❏
   b) Indigestion or heartburn ❏
   c) High blood pressure ❏
   d) Believing you are a failure, bad or ugly ❏

2. Which of these psychological signs of stress might you pick up on in the workplace?
   a) People avoiding making decisions ❏
   b) Staff making poor or irrational judgements ❏
   c) Work colleagues denying a problem exists ❏
   d) All of the above ❏

3. With regard to the autonomic system, which of the following is not part of the sympathetic nervous system response?
   a) Decreased digestion ❏
   b) Decreased clotting ability of blood ❏
   c) Increased breathing rate ❏
   d) Increased heart rate ❏

4. Similarly, which of these is not a true statement relating to the parasympathetic response?
   a) Pupils are dilated ❏
   b) Hearing is less acute ❏
   c) Skin is dry, hair normal/flaccid ❏
   d) Muscles are relaxed ❏

5. Which of the following is unlikely to be a significant factor relating to depression?
   a) Family or personal history of depression ❏
   b) Life-changing events such as death of a child or spouse ❏
   c) Moderate consumption of alcohol ❏
   d) Chronic pain or illness ❏

6. Which of the following is not an event likely to trigger post-traumatic episodes?
   a) War ❏
   b) Natural disaster ❏
   c) Witnessing a fatal car accident ❏
   d) PowerPoint failure during an important presentation ❏

7. Which of the following is not a characteristic of obsessive compulsive disorder?
   a) Excessive hand washing ❏
   b) Keeping lists as a reminder of tasks to complete ❏
   c) Regular checking or cleaning ❏
   d) Preoccupation with violent or religious thoughts ❏

8. Which of the following temporal events is not recognized as influencing biological cycles?
   a) New Year celebrations ❏
   b) Changing of the seasons ❏
   c) Crossing multiple time zones ❏
   d) 24-hour cycle of day and night ❏

9. Why is it important to identify your own triggers, symptoms and levels of stress?
a) To be an example to others of how to cope ☐
b) To set challenging targets for yourself ☐
c) To see warning signs and take action to ensure that symptoms do not become serious ☐
d) To know when to book your holiday ☐

10. Which of these may be negatively impacted by stress in the workplace?
a) Employee loyalty, commitment to work, productivity ☐
b) Accidents and sickness absence rates ☐
c) Brand and reputation ☐
d) All of the above ☐

TUESDAY

Job roles, responsibility and level of control

The old adage that prevention is better than cure holds true for managing stress at work. Now we have learnt what stress is and some of its effects, we can start to look at ideas, methods and practical examples of how to prevent stress in the workplace.

Today we will look at how lack of clarity around job roles, the failure to communicate or have an agreed understanding of what individuals are expected to do and the boundaries of their responsibility can lead to confusion, worry and stress. We will also consider how conflicting expectations can lead to frustration and errors.

We will learn how engaging with employees, allowing them freedom to determine how they work and the opportunity to get involved in decision-making processes can increase motivation and productivity, create a sense of power and ownership and reduce anxiety and stress.

The Dalai Lama once said:

> *If a problem is fixable, if a situation is such that you can do something about it, then there is no need to worry. If it's not fixable, then there is no help in worrying. There is no benefit in worrying whatsoever.*

Role clarity

Role clarity is about communicating clear expectations of what is to be done or achieved and the boundaries of responsibility. This is essential to reducing stress in the workplace.

Without understanding exactly what is expected of you, it is easy to be blamed for something you have done but that management felt you didn't have the authority to do, seemingly being punished for taking the initiative when things go wrong. Alternatively, you may also be blamed if you didn't complete an activity that management thought you should have done – e.g. being challenged as to why you didn't foresee a problem and take the initiative to solve it. Working in these circumstances you seem to be damned if you do something and damned if you don't.

Often you will also find that where there is an absence of role clarity there can be a considerable lag between a problem and its discovery. For example, a contractual or equipment specification change may be made and only discovered by management many months later when a dispute arises or the equipment has been installed and is found to be inappropriate. Inevitably an investigation more akin to a witch-hunt will ensue and all involved will try and point the finger elsewhere.

I am reminded of a simple story that illustrates the point on role clarity very well.

You have heard the story about Anybody, Nobody, Somebody, and Everybody?

An important job had to be done and Everybody was sure that Somebody would do it. Anybody could have done it, but Nobody did it. Somebody got angry about that because it was Everybody's job. Everybody thought that Anybody could do it, but Nobody realized that Everybody wouldn't do it. It ended up that Everybody blamed Somebody when Nobody did what Anybody could have done.

Language can also be a significant issue in role clarity; it is all too easy to write job descriptions or make statements that can be interpreted in more than one way. So it is important to avoid ambiguity and things that can be interpreted or taken out of context.

SO, NO BEATING ABOUT THE BUSH —
SOMEBODY DEFINITELY OUGHT TO
DO SOMETHING, AND
SOONISH

On Saturday we will look at time management and the importance of prioritization. You can see that without role clarity and a true understanding of who is expecting you to do what, it is hard to assign priorities and allocate time appropriately.

All roles in an organization need to have a formal job description explaining what the role is for, what is expected, boundaries of responsibility and also cover any required knowledge or training. This should be agreed by both parties. Most people get a job description when they start a new job or join a new organization but over time you get asked to take on new responsibilities and the workplace may change, and bits of what you did may transfer to others or disappear because procedures or the technology has changed. A formal job description should never be used as a barrier to taking on or changing your duties but it should be reviewed regularly to make sure it stays current and meaningful.

Role conflict

When we talk about conflict we usually think about disagreements between two parties and this may occur in the workplace (we deal with this on Thursday). Here we are thinking about conflict within an individual's role. There is a potential for stress when two parts or elements of a job are seemingly incompatible. As a parent of small children this is something you have to wrestle with on a daily basis. On the one hand you need to encourage your children to be honest and open and confident that they can confide in you, on the other there is a need to provide discipline when you find out something naughty has been done, thus discouraging the open and honest behaviour you are seeking to instil.

Work examples may include potential conflict between productivity over safety, or company loyalty over care for subordinates. Think of a medical doctor: they have to balance care for the individual patient with getting a certain volume of appointments completed in each day.

The most obvious solution is to deconflict a particular role, by designing jobs and allocating conflicting responsibilities to different people. While this may be practical in some organizations, particularly where the potential of role conflict can have catastrophic effects, such as safety critical roles in the nuclear or aviation industries, for many, role conflict has to remain part of the job and work becomes a balancing act to manage these conflicts.

In addition to role conflict inside the workplace, there may also be conflict from outside. The most common is the balance between work and home life. Parents have responsibilities to their family, perhaps there may be a sick or elderly relative at home or some workers may have more than one job.

Where role conflict can't be avoided and regardless of the source, these factors need to be considered and dealt with in an open and sensitive manner. I am a believer that bad news is in fact good news when delivered early. Knowing about a problem sooner rather than later allows you to deal with it before it gets out of hand. It is therefore important to provide a mechanism where people can express concern or validate their decision-making. One method is through the implementing of a **just culture** (see Thursday) where it becomes the organization's normal practice, within defined boundaries, to raise concerns and problems without the fear of punishments or reprisal and all employees have a clear authority to STOP, particularly if a problem relates to safety, quality or spiralling costs.

Being able to stop or raise issues without the fear of punishment or retribution prevents employees masking genuine mistakes or covering up problems.

Motivation

An understanding of motivation is important for any manager to get the most out of your team. It also has a direct link to stress in the workplace. If you feel undervalued, overlooked or stuck in a dead-end job, you are likely to look negatively on things and become susceptible to stress, particularly if you feel powerless to change your situation.

In 1943, Abraham Maslow presented his paper 'A Theory of Human Motivation' in which he described stages of growth through a 'hierarchy of needs'. This hierarchy of needs is often depicted as a pyramid with basic or physiological needs (air, food, water, shelter, etc.) at the base and self-actualization (the state of achieving your true potential) at the top.

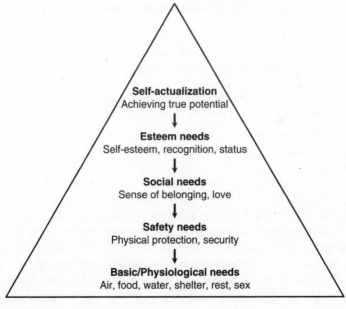

Maslow's hierarchy of needs

Maslow's model has been adapted and updated a number of times and a revised model from the 1990s is shown below.

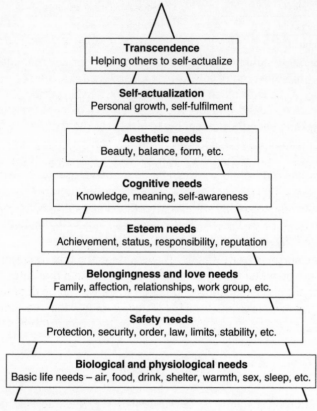

Adapted hierarchy of needs

Frederick Herzberg proposed the Motivation-Hygiene Theory, also known as the Two Factor Theory, of job satisfaction in the late 1950s following extensive research, where he investigated the factors that lead to employee satisfaction and dissatisfaction (see Table 3.1).

He discovered that certain factors were expected to be met in order to avoid dissatisfaction. These hygiene factors need to be present and well managed essentially to maintain a neutral level of satisfaction and have to be addressed before

Table 3.1 Herzberg's Two Factor Theory

Motivators	Hygiene factors
Challenge	Salary and other benefits
Responsibility	Working conditions
Promotion	Safety arrangements
Interesting or stimulating work	Security
Recognition	Quality of supervision
Achievement	Interpersonal relationships
	Status

considering the factors that result in positive satisfaction. The factors having a positive effect are described by Herzberg as 'motivators'.

Herzberg also proposed the idea of job enrichment to improve satisfaction. This involves empowering employees to take greater control of their work through less supervision, freedom to select methods and approach to work.

One surprise from Herzberg's work might be that money (i.e. pay and benefits) is a hygiene factor rather than a motivator. Herzberg himself acknowledged that there was some degree of disagreement over this point but stated, 'viewed within the context of the sequences of events, salary as a factor belongs more in the group that defines the job situation and is primarily a dissatisfier'.

As a manager, it is often easy to try and retain staff by simply paying them more, but this actually has little impact in the long-term, despite what the individuals themselves may say. As with other hygiene factors though, the expectation is that pay is as least in line with the market to avoid dissatisfaction. If this requirement is met effective managers need to seek to provide true motivators in the work environment.

Level of control

From the work of Maslow and Herzberg, we see that we have certain basic needs and other more complex motivational needs. Lack of, or failure to meet, either of these can lead to stress. Staff should be able to influence decisions and understand the reasons why, when factors are more rigid and less negotiable.

Lack of control can affect morale and self-worth and create frustration, whereas giving people greater freedom and a sense of self-determination over their place of work can encourage them to develop new skills, to undertake more challenging work, use their skills to be innovative and become more productive.

Job enrichment can be achieved by reducing supervision or allowing greater autonomy to employees to decide how they work. This approach should be supported by clear responsibilities and accountability and aligns well with an objectives-based approach to working.

It must be recognized though that some jobs (e.g. those of a repetitive nature) are less adaptable and so alternative methods need to be found to motivate employees. Here, increasing the responsibilities of staff to cover a wider remit will help to provide challenge. Alternatively, job rotation can provide variety which is beneficial both to individuals in terms of job satisfaction and the organization in terms of preventing mistakes. When engaged in repetitive and monotonous tasks employees can become complacent, distracted or blinkered to what is happening, essentially 'switching to auto pilot', which can lead to errors or accidents affecting safety, quality and productivity. Creating a sense of team and allowing for job rotation can ensure people remain focused and mutually supportive with collective responsibility for a series of tasks.

As an example, think of a manufacturing line with several stages, each requiring an operator with a specific skill. By training all the staff on the line to perform all tasks (multi-skilling), collectively the team can own the output from the line and freely rotate between positions to provide working variety. Multi-skilling may require an investment in training but this is usually outweighed by the benefits in motivation and productivity. Multi-skilling also means less reliance on individuals and a greater ability to accommodate leave, absences, etc.

In a previous role I was responsible for ride operations at a theme park. The larger rides would need a number of staff to operate, some managing queues, others batching, loading and unloading guests from the ride, looking after bags and an operator to start, stop and monitor the ride. Many of the positions required repetitive actions and had a safety dimension. Multi-skilling and job rotation proved very effective in ensuring safety was maintained but also by providing variety for employees they remained motivated and as a consequence interacted better with guests, improving the quality of their day out.

Objective output-based working

Objective output-based working means providing less prescription to employees and supports an increased level of autonomy and control. Mutually agreeing a specific work outcome and allowing the employee freedom to determine how to achieve the objective in a specific timeframe addresses many of the motivation factors identified by Herzberg.

A common acronym for effective objective setting is SMART:

- **S**pecific
- **M**easurable
- **A**chievable
- **R**elevant
- **T**imely or **T**ime bound

SMART work objectives provide clarity by defining **S**pecifically what needs to be accomplished, the reasons why, who is involved and any specific requirements, boundaries or constraints. The **M**easures of success define how much or how many and a clear end point, i.e. how you know when you have achieved the objective. They must be **A**chievable, which means providing stretch and challenge to an individual or team but not so extreme to be unrealistic. Objectives must have a **R**elevance to an individual or team and the organization as a whole, otherwise it is hard to understand the context and value of what is to be done. A clear **T**ime constraint provides a guide as to the level of urgency and the prioritization of tasks.

Regarding the relevance of objectives, this is one area that is often overlooked as obvious, but failure to adequately think through the consequences of an objective can force actions and behaviours that may be counterproductive. An example is objectives for an organization's sales force. While it is obvious the sales team should sell more, if volume is the only measure of success, it will drive sales at any cost, reducing profit margins or even selling at a loss. Also the sales team may sell more than can be delivered, leaving customers disappointed or a workforce burnt out trying to deliver more than they can produce. So relevance needs to be assessed in a broader context.

Employee engagement and consultation

In many situations there are statutory requirements to consult with employees on a variety of matters. Irrespective of external requirements it makes good sense for managers to engage and consult with their staff, ensuring that everyone has a voice in influencing their work practices and environment. The ability to influence decision-making provides a feeling of power rather than powerlessness; as we have learnt, being powerless to impact your situation or surroundings plays a key part in levels of anxiety or stress.

Organizations might wish to create some form of employee forum or consultation group, or utilize existing bodies such as trade unions for this purpose. There are several challenges that need to be addressed for such a group to be effective. The group needs to be truly reflective of the workforce, a balance of management and employees, and adequately representative of different departments, functions and workgroups. Usually representatives should be elected, demonstrating they have the support of their peers, and serve for a defined period of time ensuring they can step down or periodically refresh representation if ineffective.

Representatives need to have time to consult with their peers to be effective, and need to be sufficiently robust to represent views, even if they have personal feeling to the contrary. It is important to keep individual, internal or external politics out of discussions and decision-making. The most important element is to ensure that the group actually has power and that feelings and comments from employees are acted upon, and where this is not possible the reasons why are clearly explained.

Engagement groups should be able to influence both hygiene factors and motivators in the workplace. For example, they may comment on safety and operational procedures, breaks and work patterns, levels of supervision and how pay and benefits are awarded in relation to performance as well as working with management to ensure work is challenging and people receive appropriate recognition.

On Friday we will look more closely at change management. When an organization is planning significant change, whether downsizing, expanding, implementing new work practices or machinery, employee engagement and buy-in is critical for success. Therefore, the engagement and consultation structures an organization uses day to day can become a powerful vehicle to ensure a successful change.

Manager's action

An effective manager should try to minimize conflict, improve clarity and empower employees. Sometimes you may not be supported by the organization as a whole, but you can set an example within your area of responsibility. You should regularly ask yourself some questions:

- Do you discuss working practices and arrangements with employees, and act on their feedback?
- Do you discuss employees' objectives, progress against objectives and aspirations for the future?
- Do you encourage training and development and provide opportunity for progression?
- Do employees raise issues and concerns early and help identify causes and solutions?
- Do you thank and recognize individuals and teams for their efforts?

Of the above I have found nothing motivates employees more than recognition that they have done well. So say 'thank you' often and sincerely. Two simple words can reduce tension and flood the body of both manager and employee with feel-good chemicals. You will reinforce positive behaviour and build a bank of goodwill which you may need to draw on in the future. So whoever and for whatever reason, say thank you – you will find people are happy and more open, you can follow up with questions about what they have achieved, what they have learnt and what you can do to help in the future.

Summary

Today you have leant how to reduce worry and anxiety for your workforce by setting clear expectations and responsibilities for individual job roles. You saw how to reduce role conflict and ambiguity and how to provide appropriate support to staff where conflict can't be avoided, using open and honest dialogue without fear of punishment or reprisal as part of a just culture.

You have examined the works of Maslow and Herzberg, and how these theories support the idea of allowing employees to have greater freedom and control concerning their work and work environment, and learnt how to set SMART output-based objectives to improve motivation.

Consideration was given to multi-skilling and job rotation to provide variety and reduce errors and to create a sense of team or collective ownership for a series of activities or tasks. Finally you covered some principles of employee engagement and consultation and considered some simple questions you should ask yourself as a manager to ensure you get the most out of your team.

SUNDAY

MONDAY

TUESDAY

WEDNESDAY

THURSDAY

FRIDAY

SATURDAY

Questions [Answers at the back]

1. Why are clear responsibilities important?
   a) To ensure you know who to blame when things go wrong ❑
   b) To provide clarity so everyone knows what's expected of them and can manage their priorities accordingly ❑
   c) To ensure you know you are not paying someone too much ❑
   d) To give human resource the correct paperwork ❑

2. If an employee raises a concern regarding role conflict, you should...
   a) Tell your boss immediately to avoid being blamed ❑
   b) Get the employee to swap roles with a work colleague ❑
   c) Give the employee a pay rise and ask him to live with it ❑
   d) Discuss the issues and try to identify potential solutions with the employee's involvement ❑

3. In the hierarchy of needs, which needs should be satisfied first?
   a) Esteem ❑
   b) Social ❑
   c) Safety ❑
   d) Physiological ❑

4. In Herzberg's two factor theory which of the following is not a hygiene factor?
   a) Salary ❑
   b) Achievement ❑
   c) Working condition ❑
   d) Quality of supervision ❑

5. Which of the following is not a motivator?
   a) Challenge ❑
   b) Interpersonal relationships ❑
   c) Responsibility ❑
   d) Interesting work ❑

6. Which of the following is not an element of SMART objectives?
   a) Specific ❑
   b) Measureable ❑
   c) Robust ❑
   d) Time-bound ❑

7. Why might setting a volume-only sales target for the sales team become counterproductive?
   a) It might drive behaviour that was unintentional, reducing margin or exceeding production capacity ❑
   b) Human resources says everyone has to have a safety objective as well ❑
   c) We may have to pay the sales team extra commission if they meet the target ❑
   d) It wouldn't be counterproductive, increasing sales is a good thing ❑

8. Why might job rotation improve motivation?
   a) Employees get a greater variety of work and a sense of shared ownership ❑
   b) Employees get to spend more time training than working ❑
   c) Employees get to pick a job that pays more ❑
   d) Employees get to move around so no one knows who's responsible anymore ❑

9. What important factor should be considered in establishing an employee forum?

a) Make sure none of the trouble makers get elected as representatives ☐

b) Make sure you make decisions before the meeting so you can tell everyone what's happening ☐

c) Make sure all departments and functions are represented, including managers and employees ☐

d) Make sure representatives are kept busy to avoid them chatting to other staff ☐

10. What can I do as a manager to improve the motivation of my team?

a) Discuss concerns and issues ☐

b) Encourage training and development ☐

c) Say thank you ☐

d) All of the above ☐

SUNDAY MONDAY TUESDAY WEDNESDAY THURSDAY FRIDAY SATURDAY

WEDNESDAY

Workload, work pressure and work environment

It is easy to see ourselves as overworked. Sometimes this is genuinely true, other times it is down to personal negative perceptions or our own expectation of what good performance looks like, rather than being driven by management or others in the workplace. It is also easy to confuse activity for productivity. We may spend all our time travelling from site to site, in meetings or writing reports but never seem to get anything of value done.

On Saturday we will consider time management and prioritization, an important skill for managing workload and pressure, in more detail. Today we will focus on how, as a manager, you can build on knowledge from yesterday to motivate employees without setting unrealistic targets to improve workload and pressure and will learn to distinguish between activity and productivity.

We will see how you can use Pareto analysis to identify the most significant factors in order to prioritize improvement activity and will consider some lean principles, tools and techniques to help increase productivity and reduce workplace stress by removing waste, eliminating bottlenecks and smoothing work demands.

Finally we will look at how elements of workplace design and the work environment can create or contribute to work pressures and stress and we will investigate how these elements can be effectively managed.

Workload and work pressure

In the absence of clear communication of expectations, people will make assumptions based on behaviour. As a manager you may think it appropriate to always be the first one into work and the last one to leave at the end of the day. This might be required or a self-imposed demand. Either way your behaviour will set an expectation among your team. Others will pick up and mirror your practice making an assumption that because you do it it must be important and therefore if you're going to get on, that is what is expected.

This innocent action now creates an atmosphere where, potentially, people fear to ask for time off or to leave early to attend their children's school theatre production, a dentist appointment, etc. Staff may switch to auto pilot where they perceive it is more important to be seen sat at the desk, irrespective of what they are doing. Pressure mounts, resentment sets in and before long the entire office is stressed out.

This example is real, if perhaps a little extreme, and something I encountered first-hand, when a bold secretary came to see me to vent the frustrations of my team. My response was one of shock: of course I don't expect people to be there the same hours as me or miss the Christmas play. Today I make a point of varying my start and finish time so I am not always first in or last out, take an interest in what others are doing out of work and make a point of leaving early occasionally, and the impact is quite stark. We will look more at the impact of behaviours tomorrow.

As well as driving psychological expectation, as a manager you also set physical expectations. These might be production or other performance targets, contracted working hours or shift patterns. We learnt yesterday that challenge is an important part of motivation and setting SMART output-based objectives can provide employees with greater control over their working day. This work freedom also helps reduce work pressure as individuals have the power to influence how they work.

When setting SMART objectives other factors you should consider include:

● Are demands appropriate in relation to agreed timetables/ hours of work?
● Is the individual physically capable of meeting the demands?
● Are equipment or processes capable of meeting the demands?
● Are skills and abilities matched to demands – does an individual have the appropriate competencies and training?
● Have any concerns been addressed and how will issues be raised?

Productivity and process improvement

In addition to a particular manager's approach, workload and work pressure are often associated with poor processes and productivity. This might be that work isn't divided equally among staff, creating a bottleneck for certain tasks or individuals, which in turn creates a feeling of overwork, pressure and stress. Alternatively, operational procedures or authorization processes might be unnecessarily complex or have been written without the involvement of those actually performing a task. The slogan *work smarter not harder* is often bandied around by managers but few actually act on this intention. How many times have you or work colleagues said 'This job would be so much easier if we just...'

In the next couple of sections we will learn some basic tools and techniques for improving processes and increasing productivity, thereby avoiding excessive workload and pressure.

Pareto analysis

Sometimes it is hard to know where to start. A useful tool for both managing your time and tackling problems is Pareto analysis. The idea is that 80% of tasks can be completed in 20% of the time and this has clear implications for time management, which we will discuss on Saturday. Today, we can apply the same rule to work demands and productivity, assuming that 80% of productive activity can be completed with 20% of the tasks and the remaining 20% productivity taking 80% of the time or covering 80% of tasks.

Essentially Pareto analysis lets you determine where you will get your biggest impact for the time and money spent on improvement – 'the best bang for your buck!'

Sometimes you need to consider how you analyse your data. Consider the example below, a real situation I dealt with, in which you can see how powerful Pareto analysis can be.

A company runs a set of fast food restaurants in a particular town. Each of the six restaurants occasionally runs out of certain product lines of food. This causes customers to complain, and staff to become pressured as they think they might be blamed by management and will also have to deal with angry customers. They decide to solve the problem and collect data on which restaurants have the biggest problem and what the cause of the problems are, and graph their results.

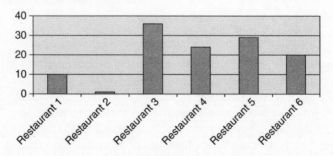

Number of product lines run out by restaurant

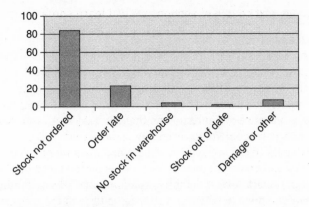

Causes of product lines running out

By simply looking at the number of events in the first graph they might choose to focus on restaurant 3 and deal with over 30 events. However, if they consider the causes across all restaurants they see that the single biggest problem is stock not being ordered. This means they can focus on over 80 events across all the restaurants, getting more from their effort. In the real-life situation, this was investigated and a simple reminder system implemented by the central warehouse. Each day they would ring round each restaurant at the end of the day to check orders had been placed in the electronic system. Problem solved, customers were happy, stressful situations for staff were removed.

Five lean principles

Terms such as Lean, Kaizen, Six sigma or Process improvement can sometimes get bandied around as management buzz words. They have been around for a number of years and all seek to improve productivity. While my personal feeling is that all of these practices can add value, you can take it too far and forget the social and people elements of work which in themselves contribute to productivity. However, the pragmatic application of some of the principles and tools can significantly improve workload and pressure and a summary is provided below.

1. Identify what adds value

Value-added activity changes something for the first time to meet a customer requirement, while non-added activity takes time and resources but does not change anything and/or does not help meet customer requirements. Here we are using the term customer to mean an external or end customer as well as an internal customer such as the next task in a production line, another department or facility.

It sounds obvious but think about your working day and how much of your time is spent on non-value added tasks such as waiting, rework, etc. It stands to reason that if you can reduce non-value added activity you will free up time to focus on other work demands and knowing that you are actually doing work that adds value can motivate you and the team.

It is important to note that some non-value activity may be essential to complete a process, but just because it is essential doesn't mean to say it has to be value-added. Don't take things for granted and don't be afraid to ask 'Why do we do this?'

In a previous job I used to spend at least two full days each month creating a very detailed operations report with dozens of graphs, dashboards and action plans. This was very demotivating and frustrating as I knew no one in head office really took any notice or rarely went beyond the summary front cover. I was wasting my time but someone long ago had decided we needed the report, so it had to be done. One month I decided to put my theory to the test and simply updated the front page and left the remainder of the report exactly as the previous month. No comments came back. When I explained what I had done to head office, the requirement for the monthly report was reduced to one page for all seven of our facilities, freeing myself and my opposite numbers at other sites to focus on other activity.

2. Eliminate waste

There are generally seven types of recognizable waste:

- defects or mistakes
- over-production

- transportation
- waiting or unnecessary approvals
- inventory or excessive stock
- motion
- over-processing.

The challenge is to reduce these in favour of value-added activity. Some examples that apply to stress management include motion and the reduction of physical labour, perhaps relying on mechanical aids rather than manpower, or perhaps unnecessary or burdensome procedures or approvals processes, that create frustration and pressure when work is 'stuck in the system'.

3. Make value flow at the pull of the customer

All too often our work rate or workflow is dictated by activities that occur prior to an activity reaching us, rather than us responding to the request of an internal or external customer. This essentially drives work rate that will find the weakest link and create a bottleneck.

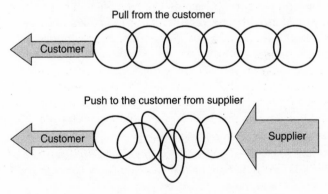

To deal with bottlenecks the temptation is to just add more resource or equipment. However, you might discover that with some simple analysis you can smooth demand across the existing resource, sharing the workload and reducing pressure on individuals.

The following real example relates to the operation of a roller coaster in a theme park that was regularly failing to meet its guest throughput target (the number of people going on the ride each hour). This affected queue times and customer satisfaction, as well as the stress of staff from pressure of failing to meet the target and potentially dealing with unhappy customers who had to queue for a long time.

The ride could theoretically be dispatched every 20 seconds (this is sometimes called takt, the available working time divided by the customer demand). To achieve this takt time of 20 seconds a number of activities or process steps had to be completed simultaneously: guest batching, bag collection, loading, ride dispatch, etc. When measured, each of these steps could be completed in the allocated time, as seen in the diagram below.

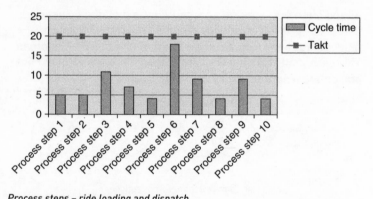

Process steps – ride loading and dispatch

Then we looked at how the ten process steps were divided among the five ride staff, the operator and four attendants, and from the load chart below, you can easily see that the bottleneck was the second attendant.

As you might imagine the second attendant position was one that no one wanted to do as they would always be seen as letting the team down – no matter what they did they were always holding the ride up. Rather than add more resource, we were able to allocate one process step each to attendants

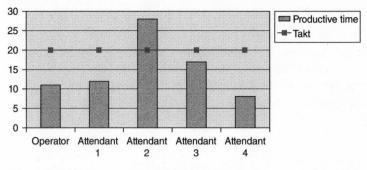

Ride staff load chart

1 and 4 from the second attendant as they were underutilized (also potentially demotivated as they spent time hanging around waiting for the second attendant).

So in the end everyone in the team was used efficiently and could work within the takt time and avoid the bottleneck, as seen in the final chart below, making both staff and customers happy.

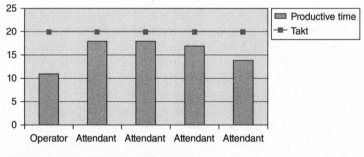

Ride staff load chart – after change

4. Involve and empower employees

When we look at change management tomorrow we will see how employee engagement is critical to successful change. We also learnt yesterday how challenge and engagement can improve motivation and create a sense of team, a buzz and energy to make things happen.

5. Continuously improve

Once improvements have been made, revisit them regularly to make sure changes are effective. Customer needs, technology, staffing and the interaction between different processes all change over time and create additional opportunities to improve the way you work to smooth demand, reduce pressure and engage and motivate the workforce.

Workplace design and work environment

Yesterday we looked at Maslow and Herzberg and learnt that basic biological needs and other hygiene factors need to be managed to avoid dissatisfaction. The work environment includes both the physical and psychological surrounding in the workplace. Therefore, designing the workplace, whether the layout of a factory or production line, right down to the way you organize your desk can play an important role in managing stress.

Ergonomics, sometimes called human factors, is the study of how humans interact with their work environment or other parts of a system. It plays an important role in workplace design to ensure that unnecessary demands or stress aren't placed on the body or mind.

Ergonomic evaluation looking at physical demands of a workplace is particularly important when jobs involve significant physical effort, sitting or standing for long periods as well as close-up or detailed work.

Ergonomics can also take into account psychological aspects. Think about the design of computer software and the frustration created if it is not 'user-friendly', the continual repetition of tasks that may lead to mistakes or poor warning signs and signals. For example, a warning light that flashes green is counterintuitive, as we usually associate red lights with danger or abnormal situations.

When considering ergonomics, the need to design workplaces so that elements can be tailored or adapted to suit the individual should be considered. This can cover everything from adjustable seating and workbench height to environmental factors such as heating, lighting, etc. After all, everyone is slightly different when it comes to their height, size, physical capability and personal preference as to what is comfortable.

The training of staff is also important so that they understand and utilize correct work methods. These might include lifting techniques, posture for standing or seating to reduce the impact of work on the body, or instructions on the use of systems and equipment.

In general, workstations or areas should be designed to:

- ensure the right tools and equipment are available
- allow for easy access of most frequently used items/tools
- avoid repetitive motions
- avoid bending, stretching, reaching and stooping
- avoid the need for transporting product by hand (use shoots, rollers, conveyors, etc.)
- be easily adapted, adjusted or modified to accommodate individual needs
- allow access for maintenance tasks and repair.

Processes tend to operate better when activities are arranged sequentially. Depending on available space this can be achieved using lines, circles or U-shaped designs. Some reorganization of the workplace can be done easily and cheaply – try using scale plans and moving furniture and equipment about to see how it might work before physically moving anything. Remember to engage with everyone who uses the workspace or area to get everyone's input and views. Clearly, if more significant change is required and at significant cost it is always advisable to get some professional support in the design process.

Tomorrow we will look at the psychological environment in terms of behaviours, social interaction and culture but today we consider some additional elements of the physical environment.

Most organizations take care of the basics of life through provision of shelter, toilet facilities, water and space to store, prepare and eat food, although in some cases provision of these essentials can be a challenge (think about those working in remote outdoor areas such as pipeline engineers, surveyors, forestry workers, etc.)

Other considerations should include:

- **lighting** – the use of daylight verses artificial light, intensity, suitability for the type of work, local bench or task lighting for detailed close-up work, changing level for night work or seasonal variations
- **heating or cooling** – variation dependant on the physical nature of work activities, ambient temperature of work environment and individual preferences
- **ventilation** – volume of ventilation to provide regular changes of air. This may be impacted by use or presence of chemicals, dust, vapours or even bad odours
- **noise and vibrations** – control of loud or excessive noise but also consider low level background noise such as equipment humming or office chatter (piped music can be both a blessing and a curse)
- **personal space** – sufficient to move about, stretch and complete work activity
- **maintenance** – consider the impact of poorly maintained or outdated tools and equipment

Playrooms and power naps

Some progressive workplaces can take design of the work environment to the extreme, making it more like home than the workplace. Playrooms encourage staff to take time out to relax from their usual work activity, play video games when things get too much and they need a release, or have a power nap. Evidence suggests that this can boost productivity, particularly in the afternoons.

Softer work surrounding such as lounge-like meeting rooms can provide a relaxed environment particularly appropriate for creative industries where innovation and problem-solving are a key part of day to day work. The relaxed environment makes it easier to think and brainstorm ideas.

This type of approach is not for everyone and is particularly popular with industries such as internet-based or software companies, marketing organizations or organizations attracting highly skilled younger workforces with a different perspective on work.

Summary

Today you have learnt how management behaviour can set expectations among the workforce that can contribute to work pressure and stress; communication and clarity are required to manage these expectations.

You considered the difference between activity and productivity and how the use of some simple tools can help identify bottlenecks and smooth workload. You learnt how using Pareto analysis can help you determine which areas are a priority for improvement and you covered the five principles of lean thinking.

You saw how workplace design can reduce stress by considering the order of tasks, ergonomics, and some simple rules to ensure ease of use and reduction of physical effort. You learnt how environmental factors such as lighting, heating and noise also play a part and considered the need to design for individual adjustments.

Finally, you saw how some organizations take workplace design to the extreme, creating playrooms to stimulate creativity and innovation.

SUNDAY

MONDAY

TUESDAY

WEDNESDAY

THURSDAY

FRIDAY

SATURDAY

Questions [Answers at the back]

1. As a manager, how might always being the first in and last out of the office negatively impact staff?
a) It might drive expectation that staff should do the same and avoid leaving early or being seen as not spending enough time at work creating pressure or stress ❏
b) Staff will resent you being good at your job ❏
c) The office cleaners will not be able to clean your office ❏
d) No negative impact, employees should follow their manager's example ❏

2. Which of the following is not a correct statement about Pareto analysis?
a) It suggests 80% of tasks can be completed in 20% of the time ❏
b) It suggests 80% of productivity can come from 20% of the tasks ❏
c) If everyone worked at 100% efficiency you could reduce your workforce by 80% ❏
d) Data may need to be viewed more than one way to see the biggest issue ❏

3. Which of the following are important lean principles?
a) Identify what adds value ❏
b) Eliminate waste ❏
c) Continuously improve ❏
d) All of the above ❏

4. Of the items listed below, which one would not be considered as waste?
a) Waiting or unnecessary approvals ❏
b) Maintenance activity ❏
c) Transportation ❏
d) Defects or mistakes ❏

5. Which negative impact might result from operating at a pace dictated by an internal or external supplier?
a) Bosses will see who isn't pulling their weight ❏
b) Bottlenecks may occur that create work pressure for certain individuals or tasks ❏
c) Internal suppliers will be able to reduce their work rate ❏
d) None of the above ❏

6. Why might continuous improvement be of value?
a) To ensure everyone is always busy ❏
b) To ensure that a new manager has opportunity to put their stamp on the workplace ❏
c) To ensure those not adapting to better ways of working are performance managed ❏
d) To ensure changes are still effective and changes in customer need, process or technology are considered ❏

7. Why might effective workplace design reduce workplace stress?
a) Changing the workplace is always seen as a positive thing ❑
b) Good design can reduce the demands placed on the body and mind ❑
c) Having chairs that adjust means people can work longer hours at the computer ❑
d) Good design can impress customers when they visit the organization ❑

8. Which of the following is an appropriate definition of ergonomics?
a) The study of human biology ❑
b) The study of how humans interact with their environment ❑
c) The study of human temporal behaviour patterns ❑
d) The study of business finances ❑

9. Which of these is not a valid consideration when assessing lighting levels in the workplace?
a) The amount of daylight coming from windows and skylights ❑
b) The ability to control/switch lighting on and off to suit individuals needs ❑
c) The level of detailed or close-up work undertaken ❑
d) Ensuring that lighting levels are the same across an entire office, building or site ❑

10. What might be the benefits of designing a more relaxed working environment, including installation of softer meeting areas or playrooms into the workplace?
a) More effective use of rest breaks to improve productivity or to encourage creative thinking and innovation ❑
b) Employees will spend less time working and will therefore be happier ❑
c) It will make use of redundant office space ❑
d) None of the above ❑

THURSDAY

Behaviours, conflict and support

So far throughout the week we have looked at a variety of topics. While each chapter stands alone you will hopefully by now have started to see how all the elements overlap to form an effective programme that will help you manage stress in the workplace.

In today's chapter we will look at how behaviours play a vital role in supporting the more procedural or physical elements of managing stress. We will look at submissive, assertive and aggressive behaviours as well as considering some classic psychological experiments that demonstrate the role authority can play in changing behaviours for both better and worse.

We will consider how management can set behavioural expectations and manage them like other performance objectives. Building on existing knowledge we will look at empowerment in more detail and consider a just culture model. Then we will examine types of internal conflict, workplace bullying and harassment as well as appropriate actions and methods of providing support.

Behaviour

Much research has been documented regarding submissive, assertive and aggressive behaviour and character traits. Table 5.1 summarizes some of the attributes relating to these behaviours.

As you might imagine, those who behave in a more submissive way may be at greater risk of bullying or harassment and may therefore benefit from assertiveness training. Likewise those exhibiting more aggressive tendencies would also benefit from coaching to consider the impact of their behaviour. As we saw on Sunday, we need to consider what we have learnt in context and avoid making judgements about individuals based on one set of observations.

In addition to personality traits such as submission, assertion and aggression, level of authority can have a significant impact on the behaviour of those with and those subject to authority. The following two experiments show just how easily behaviours can be influenced and modified in response to authority.

Table 5.1 Attributes of submissive, assertive and aggressive behaviour

Attribute	Submissive	Assertive	Aggressive
Perceived value of other	High	High	Low
Perceived value of self	Low	High	High
Approach	Submits or defends, others first, concedes easily	Respects others, both equal, negotiation	Attacks others, self first, stands firm
Speech and language	Apologetic, hesitant and avoids the real issue	Clear, concise, honest, open and positive	Threatening, accusatory, demanding, interrupts
Other visible cues	Head down, no eye contact, fidgeting	Eye contact on same level, open, balanced and relaxed	Staring, standing over or above others, hands on hip, waving and pointing

Milgram experiment

Stanley Milgram, a psychologist at Yale University conducted a study in the 1960s in response to war trials following World War Two. The study sought to examine obedience, a common defence in the trials with the accused maintaining they simply followed orders from their superiors. Milgram wanted to see how far people would go in obeying orders if it involved harming another human.

The experiment involved two volunteers (who thought they were participating in a learning study), one taking the role of a learner and the other a teacher. Finally, there was an experimenter, played by an actor and dressing in a white coat, representing a figure of authority.

The learner was strapped to a chair with electrodes, behind a screen and asked to memorize pairs of words. The teacher then tested the learner by reading one half of the pair of words and asking the learner to recall the other paired word. The teacher was told to administer an electric shock each time a mistake was made, and the level of shock increased each time, starting at 15 volts (a slight shock) and progressing to 450 volts (a severe, potentially fatal shock). No shocks were actually given but a sound recording was linked to the shock switches so the teacher heard what he thought was the learner being shocked each time.

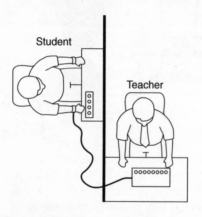

Layout of the Milgram experiment
© *Barking Dog Art*

When the teacher refused to administer a shock and turned to the experimenter for guidance, he was given a standard series of instructions:

1 Please continue
2 The experiment requires you to continue
3 It is absolutely essential that you continue
4 You have no other choice but to continue

The experiment was repeated numerous times and all the participants continued to 300 volts, and 65% of participants continued to the highest level of 450 volts. The experiment showed that people are likely to follow instructions given by an authority figure, even to the extent of killing an innocent human being. Society ingrains our obedience to authority from a young age, obeying parents, teachers, police officers and others in authority.

The Milgram experiment has been repeated in many countries since and although the percentages of teachers prepared to administer the maximum shock does vary, the overall findings remain consistent. The experiment has been criticized for its approach and methodology, even of psychological abuse to the participants.

Stanford Prison or Zimbardo's experiment

This experiment was a study conducted by Phillip Zimbardo in the basement of the Stanford psychology building in 1971, where he had created a mock-up of a prison. He aimed to study the psychological effect of being a prisoner or prison guard.

Twenty-four male students were selected and assigned roles as guards and prisoners in what was supposed to be a two-week study. Guards were dressed appropriately and given wooden batons, while the prisoners were subjected to standard processing including fingerprinting and mug shots, and were then assigned numbers which were displayed instead of names on their prison uniforms. Prisoners had to remain in their cells overnight but guards could leave when they had completed their shifts.

In a short period of time the participants had adapted to their roles to such an extent the guards started to enforce authoritarian measures and even subjected some of the prisoners to psychological torture. Prisoners accepted abuse passively from the guards and even harassed those other prisoners who tried to prevent it. Two prisoners left the experiment and the entire study was abandoned after only six days. In his finding Zimbardo concluded that the situation rather than the individuals' personalities caused the participants to behave as they had done – comparable with the result of Milgram.

We have seen from the results of both Milgram and Zimbardo that behaviour is heavily influenced by authority and situation. It is therefore important that organizations set clear expectations for behaviour and actively manage the behaviours of the workforce. We started to consider this yesterday concerning the management behaviour of being first in and last out of the office each day, creating expectation and work pressure among their staff.

Just culture

Some organizations drive a culture of fear and blame, by seeming to react negatively when things go wrong, making examples of people when a mistake is made, irrespective of whether there was a malicious intent or not. Fear of speaking out, stopping work or being seen to have made a mistake drives behaviours of covering things up, concealing the truth and lying. This inevitably means the issues will escalate and get worse until they become so significant they are no longer concealable. In fact, fear and blame cultures have been shown as significant factors in many serious industrial disasters, with multiple opportunities to have prevented fatal consequences if someone had only spoken up.

A just culture is one that recognizes normal human fallibility (we all make mistakes) and seeks to install mutual trust between an organization and its employees. So when something goes wrong the focus is on learning and prevention of recurrence rather than blame and punishment. However, a just culture does not mean no blame, rather a proportionate response. Where deliberate or wilful acts cause damage, harm or loss, individuals can expect to be appropriately managed.

A just culture requires a significant level of organizational maturity and for management to take it seriously, ensuring that those who do admit to mistakes or errors receive positive recognition and even reward for speaking up. When it comes to conflict and bullying, a just culture makes it easier for victims to raise concerns knowing they will be heard and creates an

environment where others witnessing poor behaviour can
speak out on behalf of the victim.

Managing conflict and bullying

Conflict in an organization may result for a whole host of
reasons: disagreements about operational requirements,
change, simple misunderstandings and deliberate acts
with malicious intent. In order to manage conflict or poor
behaviours, organizations should set clear expectations so
that everyone is aware of what is acceptable and what is
not. Having considered what an organization believes to be
acceptable and unacceptable, this should be communicated to
all staff. It should be made clear what constitutes bullying or
harassment along with the consequences of engaging in such
behaviour. Managers should lead by example and promote
positive behaviours in others to avoid conflict and ensure
fairness.

Physical violence, sexual advances, verbal abuse or
derogatory comments relating to gender, age, race, religion,

sexuality or disability might be obvious behaviours that should be managed. However, other more subtle forms of bullying may occur – e.g. failing to pass on information relevant for work, discriminating between individuals when allocating work tasks, or providing reward and recognition may also be considered forms of bullying.

Certain occupations, such as the emergency services, security guards or those handling complaints, are also susceptible to conflict and bullying from external sources such as customers or members of the public. Their needs should also be considered and appropriate behavioural standards communicated through signage, etc. to clarify that certain behaviours will not be tolerated.

Once expectations have been set, it is important to ensure unacceptable behaviours are reported and resolved. The type of resolution will be dependent on the severity of the unacceptable behaviour. In circumstances where there is simply disagreement or misunderstanding this can be cleared up with discussion, a sharing of views and potentially an agreement to disagree. Perhaps where comments have inadvertently caused offence or in response to an isolated malicious incident, more robust communication of the required standards may be required or some form of formal mediation between parties. More serious issues might be managed through a formal disciplinary process, including independent investigation of the facts and action, ranging from formal verbal or written warnings up to and including summary dismissal. In extreme cases, where a criminal offence may have been committed such as physical assault, it will be necessary to involve the police or other law enforcement agencies.

Employee welfare services

In addition to clear expectations and processes to manage unacceptable behaviours, organizations should consider what support services may be offered to employees. As we have learnt, good managers provide flexibility and support to those suffering from stress, regardless of the cause, whether it is work-related or not. We have already considered how those occupations with susceptibility to disorders such as PTSD should be assessed for the need for additional workforce support.

In addition to internal support for employees, many organizations provide access to external advice and support services. These usually involve some form of hotline or contact number so that employees can discuss matters in confidence and with someone independent from the organization or employer. They can then receive direct advice or be directed to other service providers for support. Services typically include counselling, health and wellbeing, legal and financial services.

Communicating clearly what support is available and how to access these services is essential, as is the need for maintaining complete confidentiality.

Managing behavioural performance

Behaviours can have as much impact on the success of an organization as any other factor. It is therefore essential that behaviours are managed in the same way as other deliverables or results. Managers should provide regular, objective feedback on both what individuals are delivering and their behaviours. Managers should also not be afraid to use disciplinary action including dismissal for poor behavioural performance. Even where an individual is seen as indispensable because of their results (e.g. the leading sales person with twice as many orders as the next best), if this person's behaviours are incompatible with those expected by the organization then removing this person is not only the right thing to do but inevitably the whole organization breathes a sigh of relief and it becomes apparent that others can step up and fill the gap – or more often realize that although the leading sales person historically got the credit his behaviours masked the work others were already doing, so the loss is minimal overall.

The performance matrix has been used in two organizations where I have worked and has proved effective in both, particularly when linked to pay and bonus awards. Rating employees by their results and behaviours allows for meaningful discussion and prompts action if issues exist in either area.

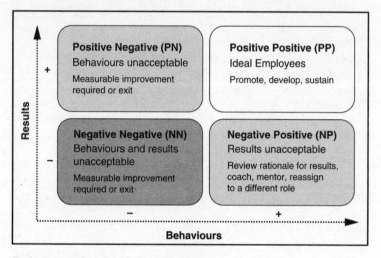

Performance matrix for results and behaviours

Summary

Today you have learnt the importance of behaviours and how these can be effectively managed. You saw how both the Milgram and the Stanford Prison experiments showed that authority can have a significant effect on behaviour, that driving a fear and blame culture can cause issues to be covered up and grow into significant problems. You considered how a just culture might aid in identifying and addressing problems early, allowing for management intervention and proportionate response.

You learnt how conflict, bullying and harassment can take many forms, some more obvious than others, and that certain people or occupations are more likely to suffer from the behaviours of others. You considered some key principles in managing unacceptable behaviours and supporting employees and gained an understanding of the pivotal role managers have in leading by example.

Finally you saw that behavioural expectation should apply equally to all and can be performance managed in the same way as other more tangible results.

SUNDAY

MONDAY

TUESDAY

WEDNESDAY

THURSDAY

FRIDAY

SATURDAY

Questions [Answers at the back]

1. Which of the following is not one of the three behaviours/character traits discussed at the start of today's chapter?
   a) Assertive ☐
   b) Submissive ☐
   c) Subversive ☐
   d) Aggressive ☐

2. Which of these are attributes of those with assertive behaviours?
   a) Respects others, high value of self and others, clear, concise and honest ☐
   b) Attacks others, high value of self, low value of others, demanding and accusatory ☐
   c) Concedes easily, low value of self, high value of others, hesitant and apologetic ☐
   d) None of the above ☐

3. What form of support might be appropriate for someone with submissive behaviours?
   a) Assertiveness training ☐
   b) Coaching to consider the impact of their behaviour ☐
   c) Self-defence classes ☐
   d) Formal disciplinary action ☐

4. What do both the Milgram and Stanford Prison experiments show us?
   a) Students are easily manipulated ☐
   b) Those in authority do what needs to be done to get results ☐
   c) Authority and situation can significantly influence behaviour ☐
   d) All of the above ☐

5. What are some of the key elements in developing a just culture?
   a) Discipline and punishment ☐
   b) Mutual trust, acceptance of human fallibility ☐
   c) No blame for anything ☐
   d) Encouraging staff to tell management about their work colleagues ☐

6. Which of the following may be considered bullying?
   a) Physical abuse ☐
   b) Withholding important work information, unfair allocation of work activities ☐
   c) Malicious comments concerning gender, race, sexual orientation and religion ☐
   d) All of the above ☐

7. Which of the following is not a means to deal with conflict in the workplace?
   a) Coaching or mediation ☐
   b) Formal disciplinary, verbal or written warnings, dismissal ☐
   c) Transferring victims to an alternative department ☐
   d) Notifying local law enforcement agencies where appropriate ☐

8. Which of the following is not an important consideration for employee support services?

a) Assessment of the most appropriate services considering the workforce needs ❏

b) Communication of what services are available ❏

c) Publicity for those who have used services ❏

d) Clear means of access to support services ❏

9. What management action might be taken for those exhibiting poor behaviours but excellent business results?

a) Formal performance management, leading to exit if no improvement ❏

b) Promotion ❏

c) Assign to a different role or department ❏

d) None of the above ❏

10. What management action would not be appropriate for someone who shows good behaviours but poor business results?

a) Understand reasons for poor results ❏

b) Promotion ❏

c) Consider reassignment to a different role more suited to skills ❏

d) Coaching or mentoring ❏

FRIDAY

Change
management

Change is a fundamental part of modern life and the pace of that change seems to continually increase. In the workplace change can happen at the organizational level through downsizing, mergers or acquisitions, privatization, contractualization or demographic change. Change may also happen at the job level with new equipment, changes to shift patterns or in reaction to short-term demands.

Change management is worthy of a book in its own right and indeed many hundreds if not thousands already exist – not to mention countless millions of internet articles and other reference materials.

In this chapter we will be focusing on the people side of change and how an understanding of people's reactions to change can lead to greater buy-in and reduced stress for management and workforce alike. We will learn how organizations and their employees have unwritten psychological contracts with each other and why people resist change. We will look at some of the many models for change, understand how engagement with stakeholders can ensure understanding of why change is needed, and how considering the views and opinions of those affected by change can deliver a better solution that staff have already invested in, making the change process easier to implement and more likely to be sustained in the long-term.

Resistance to change

Ask yourself why we resist change. Perhaps it is because of a fear of the unknown, security in the way we know, others may be resisting so people follow the pack, or some aren't convinced the change will work and don't see where the personal benefit is for them. Perhaps too much else is going on or people think it will pass like other changes that have appeared.

All these feelings are completely normal and understandable, but are often overlooked as managers simply try to force through predetermined solutions to timescales seemingly plucked from thin air. When it comes to change, it has been said that a majority of managers spend 10% of their energy selling the problem and 90% selling the solution. However, if the problem isn't properly understood then the solution won't be either.

The psychological contract

The psychological contract is an informal, unwritten arrangement built over time between an organization or employer and its employees. It represents inferred or implied obligations based

Table 6.1 Change in workers' psychological contract

Old contract	New contract
Stability	Change
Predictability	Uncertainty
Permanence	Temporariness
Standard work patterns	Flexible work
Valuing loyalty	Valuing performance and skills
Paternalism	Self reliance
Job security	Employment security
Linear career progression	Multiple careers
One-time learning	Lifelong learning

on experience and future expectation. The concept of the psychological contract is especially relevant to organizational change, in particular the move for outsourcing jobs from public to private sector, and helps us understand and plan to accommodate the reactions of the workforce.

Jamais Cascio, a writer and ethical futurist, began designing future scenarios in the 1990s. He believes that business trends drive change in order to adapt to market conditions, globalization and demands for technology to maintain competitiveness. He also suggests that change causes a shift in the psychological contract that binds workers to an organization.

Change as a transition

We can help our understanding of how change affects people by considering a few of the many models for change. Kurt Lewin proposed just such a model in 1947, and although the world has changed much since then arguably most other models are derived from the basics of his theory of three stages of change:

1 **unfreezing** – getting an organization and its people ready for change, motivating and making decisions

2 **change or transition** – implementing a new way, people are unfrozen and move towards the new approach

3 **freezing** – establishing stability in the new way

In the mid-1990s significant progress was made in change management, primarily in response to the frustrations of large organizations who continually failed to deliver sustainable change. Most of this work focused very much on the people side of change, rather than the top down methods historically used. William Bridges developed an alternative three-phase model to describe the transition.

Time

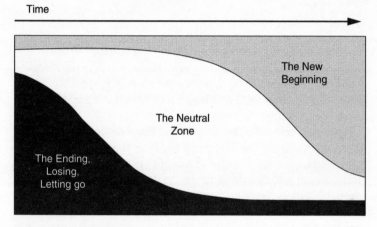

Three phases of transition

1 The first phase is an **ending**, where people are letting go. It is important to agree and sell the change, understand the impact and help people to come to terms with the loss.

2 The second phase is the **neutral zone**, where the new way isn't fully implemented and some are still working to the old way. In this phase realignment and re-enforcement are required to show progress and deal with resistance.

3 Finally there's the **new beginning**, where the change is beginning to work, energy needs to be harnessed to keep momentum going and successes need to be visibly rewarded.

Kotter's eight-step change model

In 1995 John Kotter, a professor at Harvard Business School, introduced an eight-step approach for leading change.

Step 1 – Create urgency

For change to be effective a majority of people must want it – it is important to create a sense of urgency through logical discussions on the need for and the detail of the change. People will start to talk about the change and like a snowball rolling down a hill the sense of urgency will build and grow.

Step 2 – Form a powerful coalition

In any organization there are usually one or two key players that everyone looks to for leadership. These might not be those who hierarchically are the most senior but obtaining their visible support can make the difference between success and failure.

Step 3 – Create a vision for change

People need to see what you are trying to achieve. While there may be various ideas and solutions floating around in the early days, it is important to link these into a single vision that is straightforward, easy to understand and remember.

Step 4 – Communicate the vision

The vision needs to be communicated frequently and become embedded into everything that is done. It is often easy for messages to get swamped or overshadowed in large organizations and so be relentless. Remember it is not just about what is said, people are far more likely to be influenced by what is done and others' behaviour.

Step 5 – Remove obstacles

Empower people to make the change and continually monitor for barriers, whether they are systems, processes or people. Recognize and reward those who are making progress and manage those who aren't, and help them understand the need and process for change.

Step 6 – Create short-term wins

Create short-terms targets and milestones and celebrate these successes. Success motivates people and encourages others to adopt the change. Incremental successes will also make it harder for those resisting the change as they will not be able to point to a lack of progress as justification that the change isn't working.

Step 7 – Build on the change

Real change takes time and continual re-enforcement. Declaring the job is finished too early may mean people revert back to old ways rather than continuing with new ways.

Step 8 – Anchor the change into the organization's culture

Make the change stick for good. Continue to integrate the change activity into the everyday life of the organization. Link it to reward and continually communicate ongoing successes.

Change and the personal transition

Looking back at the early models for change, we saw that individuals and whole organizations go through a variety of phases. Following research into service organizations, John Fisher's work in the naughties (early 2000s) has resulted in a very helpful model of how individuals deal with change, the process of transition curve. You can download a copy of John Fisher's process of transition curve at http://www.businessballs.com/freepdfmaterials/fisher-transition-curve-2012bb.pdf. Although consistent in its elements, the journey will be unique for each individual – some may adapt quickly, others may never fully adapt or accept change. As you read on, consider change you have witnessed or experienced and you will no doubt be able to correlate Fisher's findings with your own experience.

Anxiety

We learnt about anxiety and the feeling of unease or apprehension on Monday. In the transition process people may be unsure or feel a lack of control or visibility of a change.

Happiness

In this phase employees might feel relief that someone is doing something, satisfaction that change is coming and that things will be different from before, perhaps with feelings of anticipation and excitement. There is a risk that expectations will be raised as assumptions are made concerning what will happen and the impact. Some will think about opportunity for progression, promotion, etc. Others may think that an exit route is coming – 'they're bound to make me redundant' – and already start to spend their severance package. Thorough engagement at this stage will minimize impact.

Denial

Here people carry on regardless, 'put their head in the sand' refusing to accept that the change is happening, sticking to the old ways and ignoring anything that contradicts their view of the world.

Fear

This is a realization that things will be different in the future and everyone will need to act differently.

Threat

It dawns that the change is going to have a fundamental impact. Old choices will no longer stand. Staff may be unsure how to act in the future. Old ways are gone but new ways aren't established yet.

Anger

Anger may exist in the early stages of the transition. At first others might be blamed for forcing a change that wasn't wanted. Employees might also start to reflect on their own actions and think they should have kept control or known better. This anger at oneself can lead to guilt and depression.

Guilt

This is a realization that previous behaviours were inappropriate and that they may have had a negative impact. Being part of the problem causes a sense of guilt and sometimes shame.

Disillusionment

Disillusionment may set in if staff realize there is a fundamental difference between the individual and the organization. They become increasingly withdrawn and almost switch off, becoming dissatisfied. Recovery is possible but if the difference is too great exiting may be the only solution.

Depression

Awareness that old behaviours, actions and beliefs are no longer compatible with what employees are now expected to do or be. There may be confusion or lack of motivation as what was done and past behaviours are viewed in a negative way.

Hostility

Here, some might continue to try to make things work that have already proved a failure and others have moved on from, but they maintain the belief that it will somehow come good if they continue to plug away and ignore the new way of working.

Gradual acceptance

People start to see some of the early wins and successes of the change and start to see how they will fit into the new order. They are starting to make sense of change and acknowledge that they on the right track. There is light at the end of the tunnel.

Moving forward

Things are getting more positive and are starting to feel comfortable. Everyone is becoming more effective and understands the new environment.

Behaviours during change

We have seen above how change has distinct phases and that people go through a personal transition at a pace specific to the individual. It is important to note that while people may be at various points along the transition their behaviours may be modified by other factors – e.g.it is possible to be actively supportive of change even though you are suffering anxiety about what exactly might happen.

In the engagement and satisfaction model you will see how people may respond to a particular change in terms of their level of satisfaction and level of engagement. This model enables us to consider an appropriate management strategy for certain behaviours. Being in any one zone is perfectly normal and all are manageable; people will change their behaviours over time or in relation to different change activities.

Both axes in the engagement and satisfaction model are continuous so you will get extreme behaviours in each group. However, at the centre you tend to find those who are indifferent, those who may be easily swayed in any direction. If they see the change is happening and successful they are likely to join in, so show them the plan and keep them informed of progress. Don't be afraid to explain the dangers of 'sitting on the fence' and failing to commit one way or the other.

In the top right hand quadrant, Zone 1, you will find those who are satisfied with the change and engaged in the change process. These people can be enthusiastic and energetic and want to spread the word. Tactics for managing this group include using them to win over others and giving them plenty of support and authority to help progress the change. Make sure they are recognized, rewarded and kept motivated.

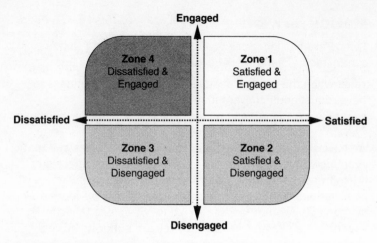

Engagement and satisfaction model

At the opposite end of the scale you have those in Zone 3. They are unsatisfied with the change and disengaged or passive in their response, failing to get involved. They may be cynical and may play a political game, agreeing in public but creating problems, spreading rumours behind closed doors. In order to manage people in this zone it is crucial to understand why they are unsupportive and tackle them on their objections. Don't dismiss their input as they may well have seen the change from a different perspective and come up with issues that you hadn't previously been aware off. Show them the change can and is working and seek their involvement.

In the bottom right are 'the saboteurs' – those who are dissatisfied with the change and are actively engaged in their opposition, potentially trying to derail the process. Sometimes their actions may be overt, other times more subtle, such as slowing up decision-making. You will need to show you understand their concerns but be able to put your case as to why you think differently. Try persuasion to bring them round to your way of thinking and try to resolve their concerns. Avoid stooping to their level and tactics, rise above them. Ultimately you may have to confront them – the change is here and if they can't engage and help make it work then perhaps they don't have a role to play in the organization. This conversation is tough but often bears fruit. If they know you are serious they may change their view and if not, it may be best for both parties if they move on. Often everyone breathes a big sigh of relief when the issue is dealt with. The important thing is to have robust adult conversation.

Finally, in Zone 4, you find those who see things as inevitable. They are satisfied but unwilling to engage fully. This group needs lots of engagement, ask them a lot of questions, gauge their views and use their expertise. Recognize and reward them but don't take their support for granted.

Timing of change

It is important to briefly mention the timing of change – get it right and you may make things easier, get it wrong and it could be a whole lot worse.

Arguably there is never a good time to change and you can always find reasons why not to do something today when you can put it off till tomorrow. However, this shouldn't stop you giving proper consideration to objections and or alternate time scales. You will need to consider other change activity: announcing that you are going to make redundancies, implement a new computer system and relocate your manufacturing plant 50 miles up the road all at the same time, might be seen as over-adventurous and detrimental to your organization. Perhaps the computer system and relocation overlap and it makes sense to deliver them at the same time, but redundancies, particularly if these relate to efficient savings from the other projects, might be better postponed.

When working in theme parks I had to undertake a major reorganization of staff, including a significant outsource of facilities management activity. I considered long and hard the timing; we could wait till the winter maintenance period when the park was closed but risked not being ready for the start of the following season or get it over and done with while the park was open and risk impacting customers now.

After speaking with key employee representatives, we went for the peak summer season, and the restructure went without a hitch. By listening to key staff I learnt that most were expecting something anyway and that they wanted it over and done with, and that on the whole most people were so energized dealing with the day to day excitement of the park during the summer that the reorganization was not their priority. Waiting for winter would mean uncertainty for longer and the change would happen when people were already low after the season had finished, their focus switched to menial tasks of cleaning, painting, etc. and they would probably be miserable due to the bad weather and short daylight hours.

Gauging the right time is more of an art than a science and nobody gets it right all the time. Remember to listen to others, and even if you don't agree make sure people understand your reasoning.

Examples of change

In my career I have witnessed and been involved with both good and bad examples of change. Good examples include the process improvement work in the theme park reorganization I have mentioned already, while the following case study serves as a lesson in what not to do.

I was working for a US aerospace company based in London, with a sister facility in Frankfurt, Germany. One Friday a senior executive flew into Frankfurt, called a staff meeting and through a translator basically said, we're closing you down with immediate effect, don't come to work on Monday and the London office will manage everything including the disposal of the building.

Clearly this came as a shock, to the German workforce but also to my team in London as we had no prior knowledge either. The senior executive flew straight back home and left us to pick up the pieces. He had failed to understand some of the basic legal rights of the workforce as well as any understanding of the implications for all concerned. While legal challenges progressed and transitional plans devised, the German workforce continued to operate the facility for a number of weeks, openly hostile to the team from London.

Law, culture, language and customer loyalty had all been misunderstood. In the end the facility was closed, many customers were lost or moved to a new company set up by former German employees and the final cost came in at an order of magnitude more than planned, which essentially much negated the business case for the closure. Interestingly, no criticism was ever made of the executive, only of those working in Germany and London!

Summary

Today you have learnt some of the reasons why we resist change, that individuals behave differently and that this variety of reactions is perfectly normal, to be expected and can be managed.

You saw a variety of models for change, Bridges' three-phase transition, Kotter's eight-step change model and Fisher's process of transition curve, each of which provides clues as to how change can be implemented effectively. You considered engagement and satisfaction to characterize types of reaction and behaviours to change and some of the management techniques appropriate for each group.

Finally, you saw how the timing of change is critical and many factors need to be considered at the planning stage to make sure bad timing doesn't create additional management issues.

Remember change management is not an exact science, but considering the principles covered in this chapter will make the process more bearable for all concerned.

SUNDAY

MONDAY

TUESDAY

WEDNESDAY

THURSDAY

FRIDAY

SATURDAY

Questions [Answers at the back]

1. Why might people resist change?
   a) Fear of the unknown or lack of security ❏
   b) Comfortable with the status quo ❏
   c) Too busy to care ❏
   d) All of the above ❏

2. Which of these is not a true statement about managing change?
   a) A variety of behaviours and reactions to change is perfectly natural ❏
   b) Those negative about change simply don't understand it ❏
   c) People may change their reaction and behaviours through the change ❏
   d) All types of behaviours are manageable ❏

3. With regard to Cascio's work, which of the following is part of the 'old psychological contract'?
   a) Predictability ❏
   b) Change ❏
   c) Employment security ❏
   d) Lifelong learning ❏

4. Which of the following is not one of the three phases of transition proposed by Bridges?
   a) Unfreezing ❏
   b) The neutral zone ❏
   c) The beginning ❏
   d) The loss or ending ❏

5. Thinking of Kotter's eight-stage change model, which of the following is a true statement about forming a coalition?
   a) Coalitions must always be with the most senior people ❏
   b) Coalitions will only work if you offer concessions to the other party ❏
   c) Visible support from key people can make the difference between success and failure ❏
   d) All of the above ❏

6. Why are Steps 7 and 8 of Kotter's model so important?
   a) Failure to reinforce or embed change may result in people reverting back to old ways ❏
   b) The true benefits of the change may not be realized ❏
   c) New people to the organization simply adopt new ways as part of everyday working ❏
   d) All of the above ❏

7. Which is not a true statement about Fisher's personal transition model?
   a) The more senior a person is the quicker they transition ❏
   b) Each individual takes a unique journey through the transition ❏
   c) Some people may miss stages of the transition, other may never accept change ❏
   d) Some people may feel guilt over the way they have previously acted ❏

8. Which of the following is a classification of reactions/behaviour to change?
a) Zone 4: Dissatisfied and disengaged ❏
b) Zone 3: Disorganized and empowered ❏
c) Zone 1: Satisfied and disengaged ❏
d) Zone 2: Satisfied and endangered ❏

9. What management tactic should not be used for those who are dissatisfied but engaged?
a) Have robust adult conversations ❏
b) Avoid adopting their tactics ❏
c) Try persuasion to bring them round to your view ❏
d) Give them a role to lead the change ❏

10. Which of these is not an important consideration when planning the timing of a change initiative?
a) The presence of other change initiatives ❏
b) Customer demands ❏
c) Being seen to make a quick impact in a new job ❏
d) Proximity to holiday times or cultural festivals ❏

SUNDAY

MONDAY

TUESDAY

WEDNESDAY

THURSDAY

FRIDAY

SATURDAY

SATURDAY

Personal responsibility and actions

No matter who you are or what you do, life can be stressful. So far in this book we have learnt about stress, its symptoms and what organizations can do to reduce and manage stress. At an individual level it is important to understand the specific triggers or activities that cause you stress and using the information we covered on Monday be able to recognize the signs of your response to stress and finally to understand what control strategies are effective for you.

In this chapter we look at some simple steps you can make to take responsibility for managing your own stress levels regardless of the type of organization you work for and the attitude of that organization towards effectively managing stress.

Much of what is discussed in this chapter may seem very simple and to some extent just common sense: manage your time, get regular exercise, and watch your diet and how much your drink or smoke. As is often the case, the simple things can be some of the hardest to do, they get overlooked by other more exciting options or it simply takes too long to embed them into our behaviours. So read on, and congratulations if you already do some or all of these things but be open to trying something new.

SUNDAY

MONDAY

TUESDAY

WEDNESDAY

THURSDAY

FRIDAY

SATURDAY

Make it a habit

Small changes in lifestyle and the choices you make can have a big impact, and quite often these changes are incredibly simple, such as take more exercise, eat more healthily, drink less alcohol. But we often struggle to maintain our discipline and soon revert to old ways of behaving. We looked on Thursday into behavioural change and although actions appear straightforward you need to make a positive effort to embed them in your daily life so that they become habitual. I took up running a few years ago and the first few weeks were really tough – making the conscious effort to get up early, stretch, warm up and run, warm down, all before hitting the shower and starting my normal daily routine took real will power. After a few weeks, with positive support from my wife and focusing on the positive benefits of losing weight and having more energy during the day, it became easier to the point where the daily run was as much a part of the routine as the shower, no longer requiring thought or effort. The same will be true for any of the suggestions in this chapter.

Be positive

At some low point in your life someone will no doubt have said to you don't worry, there's always someone worse off than yourself. On hearing this, a usual response is that people don't understand what you're going through or it may even spark a stronger response, as although probably true (statistically it is highly unlikely that you happen to be the human being who genuinely has got the worst possible life) it doesn't actually help.

That said, you might want to consider this quote from Marcus Aurelius Antonius, Roman Emperor A.D. 161–80:

If you are distressed by anything external, the pain is not due to the thing itself, but to your estimate of it; and this you have the power to revoke at any moment.

When stressed we often can fall into negative feelings or 'mind traps' that can lead to self-criticism and become self-perpetuating to the point where you eventually believe that your negative perception of yourself is in fact reality. By being aware of these thoughts, when they arise you can help yourself break the negative spiral. Common negative thoughts include the following.

Seeing extremes

The thought that 'one mistake' will result in total failure. Everyone makes mistakes and on the whole most are easily recovered. Unless you have been wilfully negligent most organizations have a formal policy of helping you improve and at least a verbal and formal written warning before it comes to the boss letting you go.

Over-generalization

If you find yourself saying 'this always happens', just pause to consider the real evidence. When emotions run high it is all too easy to shoot from the hip and ignore the facts. Think of the average married couple – at some point over a 40-year partnership one or other party will forget a birthday, anniversary or dinner date. Inevitably the focus is always on the one time you forgot rather than the 99 times you remembered and had a great time.

Rejecting the positive

You receive a compliment with a small note for improvement on the end – e.g. your boss says, 'That was a great project, delivered on time and on budget and the team really appreciated your leadership, well done. Next time I'd appreciate a bit more communication to me of potential risks to the programme.' All you hear is that the boss didn't think you communicated with him enough.

Learn to listen, acknowledge the good done and accept positive praise. If you manage others there's a lesson here, for you. Keep praise separate from criticism as people tend to focus on the latter.

Jumping to conclusions

You respond to information by making assumptions based on your perception of yourself. For example, you hear a rumour that the department is going to be reorganized and some people will be made redundant, so you instantly think this will be you. Just consider the evidence and you might actually see how a critical skill or knowledge makes you far more indispensable than your colleagues.

Time management

Rather like change management there is a plethora of programme and self-help books to help you better manage your time. Most are based around the need to:

● create an appropriate work environment
● set priorities
● perform tasks or activities against the set priorities
● minimize the time spent on non-priorities.

We touched on some organizational elements of time management on Wednesday when we looked at workload, work pressure and the work environment (e.g. value and non-value added activity, Pareto analysis and workflow analysis) but you can apply some simple rules to make your personal time management more effective.

Prioritize

Prioritization is key to time management. I use a very straightforward questioning system based on the 4Ds: Do it, Defer it, Delegate it or Drop it.

Does this activity need to be done by me and does it need to be done now? If the answer is yes to both questions is has to go in the **Do it** pile. Sometimes you have to really challenge yourself: do you have some unique knowledge, skill, experience or authority that means it has to be you?

Think about the time pressure and who this is being driven by. You might be being chased for a piece of work but you know that that it is going to sit on someone else's desk for two weeks because someone else is on vacation or the next approvals committee isn't for a fortnight. If it has to be done by me, but the time pressure isn't critical then the work goes into the **Defer it** pile. I will do it, just not now. Clearly, as time moves on 'defer it' items eventually make their way into the 'do it' category.

If someone else can do it, either now or later, then **Delegate it.** You will need to provide some guidance on the level of urgency as the person you delegate to may need to prioritize your requests with others from different sources. Make sure they understand their accountability and leave them to get on with it. Be prepared to let them make the decision to delegate it further but hold them to account for any deadline agreed.

Finally, if is not important for you to do and no one is going to be chasing anytime soon simply **Drop it.** A word of caution – make sure the originator of a task or activity knows that you have dropped it. You don't want it to come back and bite you in six months' time because they made an assumption it was still on your radar.

Effective meetings

When it comes to time management, I have found the best way to free up more time is to have effective meetings. I used to spend a significant proportion of my time in meetings – meetings that seemed to have no purpose, or that felt like repeats of other meetings I'd already attended and ones I'd leave not knowing whether a decision had actually been made or not.

Poor meetings can create uncertainty, blur responsibility and accountability and lead to confusion, particularly for those who weren't there. It is also worth remembering that they cost money. Next time you are in a meeting, consider the hourly rate of everyone round the table, add it together and see what it is costing per hour – you are likely to be shocked.

Every meeting should have a chairperson to take control, and all attendees should follow some simple rules.

Responsibilities of the meeting chairperson

- Start on time.
- Make sure all phones and unnecessary IT equipment are off.
- Have a time-bound agenda – no agenda no meeting.
- Confirm the purpose/objective of the meeting.
- Check attendees can make a contribution.
- Control the discussion and keep to time.
- Summarize actions.
- Conclude with a discussion on what went well, opportunity for improvement and what needs to be covered next time.
- Record the outcome, log and circulate minutes/records of actions.
- Finish on time.

Simple rules for all attendees

- Be on time.
- Be prepared (read reports/papers circulated in advance and have any questions ready).
- Know the agenda.
- Contribute effectively (if you can't contribute, don't attend).
- Help solve problems.
- Be respectful of others' opinions.
- Keep to the point (don't get side-tracked by discussions that aren't on the agenda).

- Make notes.
- Follow up actions.

Like any other form of behaviours, these rules for meetings need to be adopted and linked to performance reviews.

Say no

Everyone is an adult and in order to prioritize and limit the workload you have to learn to say no. Think back to the common mind gaps: how often do you say to yourself, I can't say no or I will get into trouble? If you say yes to tasks or activities most managers or colleagues assume you have given it conscious thought and have decided you can accommodate the request.

People in authority often don't see stress, particularly if people are good at hiding the signs. They may think you are very capable and because you keep saying yes keep giving you more to do. Say no, and when you have said no once you will find that people understand and will respond by saying 'Ok, no problem, I'll get John to do it instead' or they might give you additional information and provide assistance in determining what the priorities are. Try saying no but following up with 'but I can if you help me by taking on a task for me or by helping me to prioritize your request against all my other demands'.

Working from home

A regular time management action I take is to avoid commuting. Over the past decade I have changed jobs a number of times and have commuted for anything up to two hours to get to the office. Time in the car, on a bus or train can be helpful and allow for thinking time or act as a break between work and home life but on the whole, in the absence of a need for face to face contact, it can be a waste of time and money just commuting 'to be in the office'. Even if you don't have the space to work from home you might consider other local places to work from – e.g. the local library, or nearby offices of a subsidiary organization. These days the technology exists to work from home – the challenge here is discipline, and you might find it helpful to consider the pitfalls of working from home that can make it counterproductive.

First, make sure the technology works. Remotely connecting to work systems can be fraught with problems if you don't have the right equipment and technical support. Second, make the work environment right. Home can be very distracting – home comforts such as the lounge to relax in with your tea or coffee, raiding the fridge and 'five-minute' breaks to watch TV, walk the dog, etc. can all become a drain on your productive time. Working from home can also work the other way with constant access to work encroaching on your family or home life.

Create a clear work place and stick to clear work times, avoiding distraction and the blurring of the work-life boundary.

If necessary you might want to create an artificial commute, say a short walk round the block just to mentally separate your time in the home office from time with the family.

Personal health and wellbeing

In addition to positive thinking and better time management, general wellbeing and personal health have an important part to play in both combatting stress and mitigating the psychological and physiological effects. Certain illnesses, health problems and even our genes may predispose us to particular stress responses so taking care of our mind and bodies is essential for successful management of stress, but also as part of a happy, long and fulfilled life.

Activity and exercise

Life is getting more sedentary, we are collectively spending longer in cars, sat at desks or in front of the TV or a variety of other electronic devices. Studies have shown that those with higher levels of activity in their lives live longer than those less active and have a better quality of life, improving heart and lung functions and bone health while reducing blood pressure and the risk of a variety of health conditions. Physical activity includes time spent on leisure activities such as walking/ hiking, swimming, dancing, games and sports; transport activities such walking and cycling; and daily tasks such as physical paid work, household chores and community activity.

Activity is split into aerobic exercise (that which increases heart and breathing rates and involves low to moderate intensity over longer periods) and anaerobic exercise which helps build muscle with short periods of high-intensity activity.

The World Health Organisation (WHO) has issued guidance on appropriate levels of physical activity for three age ranges: 5–17 years, 18–64 years and 64+:

- Children aged 5–17 should complete at least 60 minutes of moderate- to vigorous-intensity activity daily.
- Adults aged 18–64, should complete at least 150 minutes of moderate-intensity aerobic physical activity throughout the

week or do at least 75 minutes of vigorous-intensity aerobic activity throughout the week or an equivalent combination.

- Aerobic activity should be performed in bouts of at least 10 minutes' duration.
- For additional health benefits, adults should increase their moderate-intensity aerobic physical activity to 300 minutes per week, or engage in 150 minutes of vigorous-intensity aerobic physical activity per week, or an equivalent combination.
- Muscle-strengthening activities should be done involving major muscle groups on two or more days a week.
- In addition older adults, with poor mobility, should perform activity to enhance balance and prevent falls on three or more days per week. When older adults can't do the recommended amounts of physical activity due to health conditions, they should be as physically active as their abilities and conditions allow.

When we talk about exercise we might think about signing up to a gym or contemplate investing in lots of training equipment or a personal trainer. While these are fine, you can start simply and for free. Likewise we may complain we just don't have the time but again you can start to make a real impact by some minor changes to your routine. Try taking the stairs rather than the lift, go for a walk in the park or round the block instead of spending lunch sat in the staff room or at your desk, and get off the bus a stop early and walk into work.

In addition to the physical benefits, taking up a physical hobby or sport that can be done with others or in a social group or club can improve mental wellbeing and create a vital social network of friends and support.

Diet

A healthy diet consists of the right mix of foods and the right amount. For the average person, a balanced diet consists of 33% fruit and vegetables, 33% carbohydrates from bread, pasta, rice, etc., 15% milk and dairy products, 12% protein (meat and fish) and 7% fats and sugars. Salt intake should also be limited as this has an effect on blood pressure.

In terms of amount this is best represented by the energy supplied by the food in calories. Recommended levels for calorie intake are 2,500 for men and 2,000 for women, although these are averages and the energy needs of individuals will vary dependant on age, lifestyle and size. Larger people and those with physically demanding work or leisure activities will require more calories and a more tailored diet.

Alcohol

Alcohol is a drug and it affects the body in a variety of ways. Over time and with prolonged exposure, like other drugs it can become addictive. As with certain foods that pose a health risk, it is a case of everything in moderation.

Certain professions, usually those posing particular stresses on staff through high expectation or pressure to perform, are seen as drinking professions – e.g. journalism, legal professions and corporate/investment banking – and there is often significant peer pressure for work colleagues to drink, particularly after work.

Individual governments and health agencies provide guidance on the level of alcohol consumption deemed 'safe' for both men and women. There are a variety of values, which reflect the level of uncertainty from research regarding what levels may have an adverse effect on health. Likewise local agencies will set alcohol limits for driving and other activities which are legally enforced so it is always advisable to check local data sources, particularly if travelling or working overseas.

Relaxation

Relaxation is a very personal thing, whether snuggling in an armchair with a good book, a long hot bath, lying in the sun on a summer's day, having a massage, aromatherapy or any one of a variety of formal meditation and or breathing techniques.

Care should always be taken to make sure you take a break from work. Holiday entitlement is there for a reason. Even if you don't go away and stay at home, the break gives you time to unwind. Make sure you take an 'unplugged' break – the temptation to access work in the evening or while on holiday is made all the easier by the plethora of electronic devices that give us instant access to e-mails, work networks, etc. Try to avoid this when away from work; if it is essential you maintain contact with the office when on holiday, allocate specific times to work so you can focus the remainder of your time on you, your family and friends.

Summary

You should now know that in order to cope with stress in your own life you need to:

- recognize the existence and the signs of your response to stress
- understand the specific triggers or activities that cause you stress
- understand what control strategies are effective for you.

Today you have considered how you can place demands on yourself though negative feelings and 'mind traps', how you might reduce work pressures and demands through better prioritization by deciding to Do it, Defer it, Delegate it or Drop it as well as looking to reduce commuting by working from home and to make the most out of meetings.

Finally you learnt about the importance of your personal health and wellbeing, considering the importance of regular exercise, a balanced diet and reducing alcohol intake as well as the need to understand the best way for you to unwind and relax.

SUNDAY

MONDAY

TUESDAY

WEDNESDAY

THURSDAY

FRIDAY

SATURDAY

Questions [Answers at the back]

1. Which of the following is a mind trap that can cause you to create demands on yourself?
   a) Seeing extremes ☐
   b) Over-generalizations ☐
   c) Jumping to conclusions ☐
   d) All of the above ☐

2. Which of the following statements about 'saying no' is likely to be true?
   a) My boss will fire me ☐
   b) You'll never be asked to undertake a new challenge again ☐
   c) People will understand, will ask someone else or help you prioritize their requests ☐
   d) Your work colleague will think you are not pulling your weight and shun you ☐

3. Which of these is not one of the 4Ds for better prioritization?
   a) Do it ☐
   b) Delegate it ☐
   c) Deny it ☐
   d) Drop it ☐

4. Why might ineffective meetings contribute to stress?
   a) They use up time that could be spent on other priority tasks ☐
   b) They may create confusion or lack of clarity of who is doing what ☐
   c) You might feel uncomfortable/ embarrassed if invited to contribute to a discussion not relevant to you and where you have no knowledge of the subject ☐
   d) All of the above ☐

5. Which of the following is not good practice for the chairperson of a meeting?
   a) Start on time ☐
   b) Confirm the purpose or objectives for the meeting ☐
   c) Let the meeting overrun if the discussion is lively ☐
   d) Summarize actions ☐

6. Why might working from home have a negative impact on your stress levels?
   a) You can avoid unnecessary time spent commuting ☐
   b) You might blur the boundary between home and work and end up working in the evenings and at weekends ☐
   c) You can focus on work without the continual interruptions you get in the office ☐
   d) You are still contactable throughout the day, should someone need to speak with you ☐

7. Which of the following is the recommended level of exercise for an adult?
a) At least 150 minutes of moderate-intensity aerobic physical activity or at least 75 minutes of vigorous-intensity activity throughout the week or an equivalent combination ❏
b) At least 60 minutes of moderate- to vigorous-intensity activity daily ❏
c) At least 90 minutes of moderate-intensity aerobic physical activity or at least 60 minutes of vigorous-intensity activity throughout the week or an equivalent combination ❏
d) No more than 120 minutes of vigorous-intensity aerobic activity throughout the week ❏

8. Which of the following is a true statement about diet?
a) You can eat as much fat and sugar as you like providing you do more exercise to compensate ❏
b) Your ideal calorie intake will depend on age, size and lifestyle ❏
c) A balanced diet should contain at least 33% protein from meat and fish ❏
d) An average calorie intake for a woman is 2,500 per day ❏

9. Which of the following is not an important consideration concerning the intake of alcohol?
a) Local legal blood alcohol limits for driving and other activities ❏
b) The special offers on during happy hour at your local bar ❏
c) Whether you are taking prescription medication ❏
d) Peer pressure from work colleagues ❏

10. What is the best way to relax?
a) Taking a foreign holiday ❏
b) A long hot bath ❏
c) Having your in-laws to stay for the weekend ❏
d) Find out what works for you ❏

Surviving in tough times

All kinds of situations and circumstances can cause stress in the workplace, more so when times are tough. This can create uncertainty and the financial constraints on an organization may become more evident. A basic understanding of some of the methods for reducing stress in the workplace can help to allay fears, motivate employees, improve productivity and generate goodwill, helping you and others in the organization to be more positive about potential changes.

Here are ten important tips to help you through the downturn and motivate the organization to see things through.

1 Assess the levels of stress

Consider the causes of stress, who might be affected, current control measures and potential improvements. Look out for physiological and psychological signs and symptoms. Remember to gain senior management buy-in and involve the whole organization. Monitor and continuously review progress.

2 Listen

Engage and take time to understand staff problems and concerns. Everyone is an adult and everyone is human, and besides, you might learn something to your advantage. Keep personal, internal and external politics out of discussions and make sure you get a fully representative view from across the organization.

3 Say 'thank you'

Nothing motivates employees more than recognition that they have done well. Two simple words can reduce tension and flood the body with feel-good chemicals. You will reinforce positive behaviour and build a bank of goodwill which you may need to draw on in the future. So, whoever and for whatever, even if simply doing their job well, say 'thank you'.

4 Provide clear, unconflicting responsibilities and accountabilities

Where possible remove conflicting demands on individuals or at least provide a means to escalate concerns when they arise. Ensure everyone understands what is expected of them and where boundaries lie.

5 Allow individuals control over their work

Set SMART objectives and allow individuals and teams to determine how they are delivered. Consider multi-skilling to allow for job rotation and variety of tasks. Allowing autonomy and variety will improve morale and allow both individuals and teams to be in control of their own performance.

6 Manage workload and work pressure

Use lean principles to focus employees on what adds most value and ensure that work demands are aligned with individual or team capability and capacity to do the work.

7 Consider the workplace and environment

Consider simple changes that may make the workplace feel like a nice place to be. Consider ergonomics and the usability of equipment, the need for individuals to be able to make adjustments to make work more comfortable. Improve heating, lighting, ventilation and consider maintenance of equipment.

8 Manage behaviours

Set clear expectations for behaviours and manage them in line with other performance measures. Do not tolerate bullying or harassment, make sure employees are aware of what this means within the organization and the consequences of such behaviour, how they can raise or report concerns, access help and support services.

9 Manage change

Spend time understanding the problem rather than selling the solution. Treat change as a transition and appreciate that individuals will go through their own journey. Create urgency, get buy-in and create alliances, communicate continuously, celebrate short-term success, reinforce positive behaviours and embed the change.

10 Prioritize and help others prioritize. Use the 4Ds

Do it – It has to be you and it has to be now
Defer it – It has to be you but I can do it later
Delegate it – It can be someone else, make sure they know if it needs to be now or later
Drop it – No one needs to do it anytime soon

Answers to questions

Sunday: 1d; 2b; 3a; 4d; 5b; 6c; 7c;
8a; 9d; 10a

Monday: 1d; 2d; 3b; 4a; 5c; 6d;
7b; 8a; 9c; 10d

Tuesday: 1b; 2d; 3d; 4b; 5b; 6c;
7a; 8a; 9c; 10d

Wednesday: 1a; 2c; 3d; 4b; 5b;
6d; 7b; 8b; 9d; 10a

Thursday: 1c; 2a; 3a; 4c; 5b; 6d;
7c; 8c; 9a; 10b

Friday: 1d; 2b; 3a; 4a; 5c; 6d; 7a;
8a; 9d; 10c

Saturday: 1d; 2c; 3c; 4d; 5c; 6b;
7a; 8b; 9b; 10d

ALSO AVAILABLE IN THE 'IN A WEEK' SERIES

BODY LANGUAGE FOR MANAGEMENT ● BOOKKEEPING AND ACCOUNTING ● CUSTOMER CARE ● DEALING WITH DIFFICULT PEOPLE ● EMOTIONAL INTELLIGENCE ● FINANCE FOR NON-FINANCIAL MANAGERS ● INTRODUCING MANAGEMENT ● MANAGING YOUR BOSS ● MARKET RESEARCH ● NEURO-LINGUISTIC PROGRAMMING ● OUTSTANDING CREATIVITY ● PLANNING YOUR CAREER ● SPEED READING ● SUCCEEDING AT INTERVIEWS ● SUCCESSFUL APPRAISALS ● SUCCESSFUL ASSERTIVENESS ● SUCCESSFUL BUSINESS PLANS ● SUCCESSFUL CHANGE MANAGEMENT ● SUCCESSFUL COACHING ● SUCCESSFUL COPYWRITING ● SUCCESSFUL CVS ● SUCCESSFUL INTERVIEWING

For information about other titles in the series, please visit www.inaweek.co.uk

ALSO AVAILABLE IN THE 'IN A WEEK' SERIES

For information about other titles in the series, please visit www.inaweek.co.uk

LEARN IN A WEEK
WHAT THE EXPERTS
LEARN IN A LIFETIME

For information about other titles
in the series, please visit
www.inaweek.co.uk